NEW
BRIGHT IDEAS

Phonic Fun!

AGES 5-11

Jillian Harker

Author
Jillian Harker

Editor
Sue Howard

Assistant Editor
Charlotte Ronalds

Project Editor
Wendy Tse

Series designer
Joy Monkhouse

Designers
Helen Taylor
Catherine Mason

Illustrations
Gary Swift

Cover photographs
© Scholastic Ltd

Published by Scholastic Ltd,
Villiers House,
Clarendon Avenue,
Leamington Spa,
Warwickshire
CV32 5PR

Printed by Bell & Bain Ltd, Glasgow
Text © Jillian Harker 2004

6 7 8 9 0   7 8 9 0 1 2 3

Visit our website at www.scholastic.co.uk

British Library Cataloguing-in-Publication Data
A catalogue record for this book is available from
the British Library.

ISBN 0-439-97132-2
ISBN 978-0439-97132-4

All Jillian Harker poems previously unpublished.

Contents

Introduction

The introduction of the National Literacy Strategy renewed interest in a more structured approach to the teaching of reading and spelling. The Strategy acknowledges that the teaching of phonics has a central role to play. In order to master the skills of reading and spelling, children need to make the links between the sounds of our spoken language and the patterns which we use to write those sounds. While a few children make these links without difficulty, the majority will need more explicit instruction to become competent readers and spellers, and a further, smaller group of children will need additional teaching and extra practice. The teaching of phonics provides children with the basic building blocks to develop literacy.

Contrary to popular belief, a high proportion of the English language works according to rules, and the knowledge of these underlying rules can reduce the learning load for children. This book has been constructed on the basis that children need to begin by exploring the sound / pattern link in a structured way. It is based on the principle that, with appropriately chosen material and carefully cued questions, most children can be helped to understand the structure of many of our spelling rules. When such an approach is used, children begin to see patterns emerging and words no longer have to be tackled one by one.

Some of the rules for spelling in English are dependent upon the position in which a particular sound occurs within a word, or on the letter that follows a given sound. Others depend upon the sound of the vowel, with different principles applying when the vowel has a short sound to those used when the vowel sound is long, or when its sound is modified by a following letter *r*. When these underlying principles are understood, it becomes far easier to read and spell hundreds of words. Although rules are often taught to help children with the acquisition of reading and spelling skills, the logic behind those rules also needs to be made clear. This helps a child to understand, for example, that we do not remove the silent *e* for no reason when a vowel suffix is added, but because leaving it would result in a combination of vowels which would produce an unwanted sound.

This book aims to address these issues where possible; to assist teachers with explanations to enhance children's understanding that many rules have a sound, logical basis. The book is divided into four chapters:

Chapter 1 Exploring sounds and patterns
Chapter 2 Exploring and using rules
Chapter 3 Using what you know
Chapter 4 Games and puzzles.

While Chapters 1 and 3 explore and provide practice in the basic links between sounds and letter patterns, Chapter 2 aims to demonstrate that sounds can also provide vital clues to the correct choice of spelling patterns. Since different children learn in different ways, a variety of approaches is provided, including games and puzzles (Chapter 4). Activities are graded within each chapter. A heavier, though not exclusive, emphasis is placed on the skills needed for Key Stage 1 in the chapter 'Exploring sounds and patterns', and on those skills needed for Key Stage 2 in 'Exploring and using rules'. Resources needed for the activities are clearly indicated and suggestions for differentiating each activity are also given. Photocopiable sheets are provided for some activities and these are sited at the end of the relevant chapter. Where it has not been possible to provide a photocopiable sheet, but such a master may be useful, clear instructions are given for producing this.

Activities are cross-referenced when possible to indicate, for example, when a game or a practice task in another chapter can be used to reinforce a sound / spelling pattern or rule that has just been explored. Likewise, indications are given as to how knowledge acquired in a previous activity can be used to enhance a current activity.

Curriculum links for each activity are clearly designated. References to the National Literacy Strategy will help practitioners to incorporate the activities into their current planning. Although an age range is specified for each activity, linked with the appropriate stage of the National Literacy Strategy, it should be noted that activities designated for younger children would be equally suitable for older children who have not yet mastered the skills targeted or who need further practice in those skills.

It is not the purpose of this book to suggest that the patterns of the English spelling system can be wholly clarified through the teaching of phonics. This is not the case. However, this strand of teaching can play a vital role in equipping children with a body of knowledge that helps them to understand many of the underlying principles. It also forms a sound basis on which to build a broader understanding of other principles involved in the structure of English.

CHAPTER 1

Exploring sounds and patterns

AGE RANGE 5–6

LEARNING OBJECTIVE
To be able to identify sets of rhyming words.

CURRICULUM LINKS
NLS: YR, Word level 1.

Hat tricks

What you need
A copy of the poem below.

What to do
● Explain to the children that you are going to read them a poem. Ask them to listen carefully to the words at the end of each line to see if they notice anything about them. Read the following poem:

There's a cat in a hat
and it sits on a mat.
A cat in a hat?
But why?
The cat sits like that
in a hat on the mat,
so the cat can play 'I spy'.
'I spy', says the cat
in the hat on the mat,
'a big fat rat.
Oh my!'
'Oh no!' says the rat
to the cat in the hat,
'I'm off down my hole.
Bye bye!'

© Jillian Harker

● Read the first two lines of the poem again, inviting the children to tell you whether the words *hat* and *mat* rhyme. If necessary, encourage them to listen to the ends of the words in particular.
● Now, ask the children whether the words *hat* and *mat* rhyme with the word *cat*. Point out that there were lots of other words in the poem that rhymed with these words as well. Say, *I can think of another animal in the poem whose name rhymes with 'cat'. Can you tell me what it was?*
● Tell the children that you are going to read the poem again, and explain that this time you want them to listen carefully for any word that rhymes with cat. Ask them if they can miaow like a cat, and invite them to miaow every time they hear a word in the poem that rhymes with *cat*.
● Read the poem again, pausing to indicate that a rhyme is coming for the first couple of rhyming words, but then reading at a normal pace.

Differentiation
During the second reading, cue younger children to miaow by stroking imaginary whiskers each time you read a word that rhymes with *cat*. Invite older children to miaow at the words that rhyme with *cat* and to squeak like a mouse at the words that rhyme with *spy*.

See also: Three in one (p53); Families (p73).

AGE RANGE 5–6

LEARNING OBJECTIVE
To identify the initial sounds in words and to decide which words begin with the same sound.

CURRICULUM LINKS
NLS: YR, Word level 4.

Pack the case

What you need
Whiteboard and pens, or paper and pencils.

What to do
● Depending on the size of your group, draw two large suitcase outlines on either a whiteboard or paper. Draw a name tag tied to each suitcase handle. Write the name 'Sam' on one name tag and 'Tess' on the other. Read the names to the children and invite them to tell you the sound that they can hear at the beginning of each name.
● Explain that 'Sam' and 'Tess' are going on holiday, and they would like some help to pack their suitcases. Tell the children that you are going to name some items of clothing that the two girls need to pack. Say, *Sam is only allowed to pack clothes in her case that begin with the same sound as her name. What is that sound?* Ask whether Sam would be allowed to pack boots in her case.
● Now explain that Tess can only pack things that begin with the same sound as the first sound in her name and check that the children know what that sound is. Ask whether Tess could pack a tie in her case.
● Choosing items from the list of clothes below, ask the children to decide in whose case each item should be packed. Invite a child to draw the item in the correct suitcase each time.

socks	trousers
skirt	tracksuit
scarf	trainers
sandals	tie
swimsuit	t-shirt
slippers	tights

Differentiation
Each time you name an item of clothing, emphasise the initial sound for younger children and check that they are sure what that sound is before inviting them to decide the correct suitcase. Ask older children to help you compile a list of toys and to group these according to initial sounds.
Can they think of someone in the group whose name begins with the same sound as a particular group of toys?

BRIGHT IDEAS

AGE RANGE 5–6

LEARNING OBJECTIVE
To identify the initial sounds in words and link them to other words beginning with the same sound.

CURRICULUM LINKS
NLS: YR, Word level 2.

Licking lollies

What you need
The 'Licking lollies' photocopiable sheet on page 25; thin card; whiteboard; pen.

What to do
● Make one photocopy of the 'Licking lollies' sheet for each child and cut out the individual pictures. Give each child a set of pictures and invite them to spread the pictures out on the table in front of them. Go through the pictures with the children to ensure that they know what each one is intended to be (lollies; chocolate; meat; nut; grapes; bun; sweets; carrots).
● Explain that you are going to say a word that describes a way of eating something, for example, *licking*. Ask the children which sound comes at the beginning of this word.
● Invite the children to look at the pictures in front of them. Encourage them to find a picture of something that begins with the same first sound as the word *licking* and to hold that picture up. When they have done this, say, *Licking lollies – do those two words both have the same sound at the beginning?* Write the two words on the board as the first item in a list.
● Work through the other eating words from the list below, each time inviting the children to find the picture with the same initial sound. As you build up a list, suggest that the children order their pictures in the same sequence as the list.

licking lollies
chewing chocolate
munching meat
nibbling nuts
gobbling grapes
biting buns
sucking sweets
crunching carrots

● Encourage the children to help you read the list that you have made together. Explain that you will say the eating words and they must say the correct foods. Suggest that they use their sequence of pictures to help them remember which food they must name each time. Begin by saying, *We like licking...*; *We like chewing...* and so on.

Differentiation
With younger children, offer a limited choice of two pictures to choose from each time you name an eating word. Ask older and more able children to supply the name of the letter that we use to write the initial sound of each pair of words.

AGE RANGE 5–7

LEARNING OBJECTIVE
To be able to identify each letter of the alphabet, name it and suggest an object beginning with that letter; to secure the alphabet sequence.

CURRICULUM LINKS
NLS: YR, Word level 3; Y1, T1, Word level 2.

Touch, name, sound

What you need
Wooden or plastic alphabet letters.

What to do
● Choose any four sequential wooden or plastic alphabet letters from the alphabet, for example *A*, *B*, *C* and *D*.
● Invite four children to play an alphabet game with you. Ask each of the children in turn to close their eyes, then place a letter in front of them. Making sure that the letter is correctly oriented, guide their hands over it and ask them to tell you what they think the letter is, without opening their eyes. Encourage the children to describe the shape of the letter that they are holding.
● When the children have suggested a letter name, ask them to open their eyes and check whether they were correct. Now ask each of them in turn to tell you the sound that their letter makes. Then say, *Can you think of anything that begins with that sound?*
● Point out to the children that the four letters on the table all come next to each other in the alphabet. Invite them to pick up their letters and to try to arrange themselves into line, holding the letters in front of them so that they are in the correct order.
● Choose another sequence of four letters and repeat the activity.

Differentiation
Focusing on letters from the beginning of the alphabet, help younger children to trace around their letter in the correct direction with the forefinger of their writing hand, before asking them to name the letter. Provide an alphabet line to help them to order their letters correctly.

For older and more able children, use sequences from later on in the alphabet and challenge the children to think of a word beginning with their letter from a specific category, such as animals.

AGE RANGE 5–6

LEARNING OBJECTIVE
To choose the correct spelling for the final consonant in CVC words, distinguishing between two commonly confused letters.

CURRICULUM LINKS
NLS: YR, Word level 2.

Which ending?

What you need
The 'Which ending?' photocopiable sheet on page 26; pencils.

What to do
● Make one photocopy of the 'Which ending?' sheet for each child.
● Explain to the children that you are going to say some pairs of words and you want them to listen very carefully. Then say the words *bed* and *bet* clearly. Invite the children to tell you whether these words are the same or not. Ask them in what way the words sound similar and in what way they sound different. Work through the following pairs of words in the same way:

    mat / mad   pot / pod
    cup / cub   cap / cab

● Now explain to the children that you are going to say some more pairs of words and that you want them to decide, again, if these words are the same or not. Explain that this time, if the words are different, you would like them to tell you whether they are different at the beginning or at the end. Use the following pairs of words:

    sad / sat   lit / lid
    nib / nip   cod / cot

● Remind the children that the end sound of all the pairs of words was different. Ask, *Does this mean that we will write them with a different letter at the end?*
● Give each child a copy of the 'Which ending?' sheet. Point out that there are two words under each picture which look very alike. Invite them to tell you if any part of the word pairs looks different. Explain that they must decide which of the two words is the correct one for each picture. Tell them that because the words look very alike, they will have to think very carefully about the last sound in the word that they want, and look very carefully at the last letter in both words, before they choose the correct one.
● Invite the children to name each picture in turn and to circle the correct word that matches it.

Differentiation
With younger children, emphasise the final sounds in the word pairs at the beginning of the activity. Work through the sheet as a group, encouraging the children to tell you the final sound in the target word and the letter that writes that sound before looking at the word pairs and making their choice.

    With older children, omit the oral exercise at the beginning of the activity and simply point out that the children will need to be careful about choosing the word with the correct ending.

AGE RANGE 5–7

LEARNING OBJECTIVE
To correctly identify the final sounds in words and match that sound to the appropriate letter.

CURRICULUM LINKS
NLS: YR, Word level 2.

Shuffle

What you need
Three pieces of thin card measuring 5 cm by 7 cm for each child; marker pen.

What to do
● Write a clear lower case letter *b* on the first of the three pieces of card, a letter *d* on the second and a letter *p* on the third. Give each child a set of cards.
● Invite the children to lay out their three cards in a row on the table in front of them. Explain that you are going to say a word and that they should listen carefully to the last sound in that word. Say the word *rib* and invite the children to tell you the final sound in the word. Encourage the children to look at the three letters in front of them, and to push forward the letter that they would use to write the last sound in the word *rib*.
● Check that each child has chosen the correct letter, then invite them to return the card to their row of letters.

● Explain that you are going to say another word which starts like the first one but has a different last sound. Say the word *rip*, and ask the children to tell you which sound they can hear at the end of this word. Again, invite them to push forward the letter which would write the last sound in the new word.
● Work through the following pairs of words in the same way:

rib / rip	mop / mob	map / mad	lap / lad
pub / pup	cab / cap	hip / hid	lid / lip
tap / tab	cup / cub	cod / cop	rib / rid
sob / sop	pod / pop	mod / mop	bib / bid
nip / nib	bad / bap	hop / hod	rod / rob

Differentiation
Offer younger children the choice between only two letters at a time. The list above is grouped so that children can be asked to choose between p / b, p / d and d / b endings in pairs of words. Ask older children to write each word in full after they have chosen the letter for the final sound.

AGE RANGE 5–7

LEARNING OBJECTIVE
To identify where a specific sound occurs in a word.

CURRICULUM LINKS
NLS: Y1, T2, Word level 1.

Hunt the sound

What you need
The 'Hunt the sound' photocopiable sheet on page 28; pencils.

What to do
● Make one photocopy of the 'Hunt the sound' sheet for each child.
● Tell the children that they are going to play a game called 'Hunt the sound'. Explain that although they might be used to hunting for things with their eyes, in this game they have to try to find something by using their ears. They will have to hunt a sound.
● Tell the children that the sound they are hunting is the sound *m*. Make sure that you say this sound cleanly, without including an *uh* sound. Explain that this sound is hiding in words, either at the beginning, in the middle or at the end of words. Use the word *monkey* as an example. Ask the children if they can hear an *m* sound in that word, and if they can tell you where it comes.
● Show the children the photocopiable sheet. Ask them to tell you what each of the pictures represents to ensure that they know the words to use for the activity. The pictures show: milk; a swimmer; hammer; flame; worm; mouse; lamb; match; camel; mouth; broom and motorbike.
● Explain that there is an *m* sound in every one of those words. Tell the children that you would like them to say the word and listen for that sound. If they think it comes at the beginning of the word, they should put a tick in the first box; if they think it comes in the middle of the word, they should put a tick in the middle box; if they think it is the last sound in the word, they should put a tick in the last box. Invite the children to work through the sheet.

Differentiation
Let younger children work together as a group. Say each word in turn, emphasising the target sound for them. Ask older and more able children to write the letter *m* instead of a tick. Create a set of worksheets, each focusing on different sounds, or give words orally and ask the children where specific sounds occur in those words.

See also: Missing middle (p54); All change (p74);
Round and round the garden (p75); Five in a hive (p76).

AGE RANGE 6–7

LEARNING OBJECTIVE
To correctly order the lines of a poem by using rhyming patterns.

CURRICULUM LINKS
NLS: Y1, T1, Word level 1.

Pig in a wig

What you need
'The pig in a wig' photocopiable sheet on page 27; highlighter pen; scissors.

What to do
● Read the poem 'The Pig in a Wig' to the children. When you have finished, tell the children that you are going to take a closer look at all the rhyming words in the poem.
● Read the first two lines of the poem again, then ask the children which words in those lines rhyme. Explain that when words rhyme it is because the ends of the words sound the same. Say, *Let's look at the end of those words and see if they look alike as well as sounding alike. Which two letters do those words end with?* Mark the *ig* pattern with the highlighter.
● Work through pairs of lines in this way, highlighting the rhyme pattern.
● Now cut the poem up into separate lines. Tell the children that you are going to jumble the lines of the poem up and you would like them to help you to put them back in the correct order.
● Remind the children that the rhyming words in the poem had the same pattern at the end. Explain that they can use this to help them find pairs of lines that belong together. Show them the first line of the poem, pointing to the highlighted pattern. Ask them to find another line that has the same pattern at the end. If they offer more than one line, read out both lines and invite the children to decide which one sounds correct as the second of the pair in this part of the poem.
● Now suggest that they find other pairs of lines by looking for matching patterns. When the lines have been paired or grouped, read them out and invite the children to help you sort the pairs into the correct order by thinking about the order of events in the poem.

Differentiation
Find the first line of each pair, in the correct order, for younger children, and invite them to hunt for each line's pair. Alert older and more able children to the rhyming patterns but do not highlight them. Encourage them to try to sort the lines fully into the correct order before you read back any of them.

See also: Three in one (p53); Families (p73).

Phonic Fun!

Twist your tongue

AGE RANGE 6–7

LEARNING OBJECTIVE
To read a group of words with initial consonant clusters and to recognise the matching clusters in other words.

CURRICULUM LINKS
NLS: Y1, T2, Word level 3.

What you need
Whiteboard; pen.

What to do
● Write the following words on a whiteboard, asking the children to read each word as you write it:

slugs   stop   grab   plan   trot
clap   flap   crabs spot   drop

● Ask the children to look carefully at the beginning of each word. Can they notice anything that these words have in common? Help them to notice the consonant clusters and ask them to give the sound each cluster makes in each word.
● Invite the children to help you make up some tongue twisters. Tell them that you have a list of the second half of some tongue twisters, but that the beginnings are missing. Encourage the children to help you decide which of the words on the board would be the correct beginning for each tongue twister.
● Explain that most of the words in a tongue twister begin with the same sound. Ask the children which word on the board begins with the same sound as the words *slither slowly*? The sound is *sl*. When the children have given an answer, say the words together: *Slugs slither slowly*. Invite everyone to say the phrase together quickly to make a tongue twister.
● Now read each of the phrases below in turn, inviting the children to find the correct word to begin the tongue twister:

…grub greedily
…the clever clowns
…crawl crazily
…stealing stamps
…slither slowly
…a dripping drink
…a pleasing plot
…speckled spiders
…a flowery flag
…on a tricky track.

Differentiation
Emphasise the consonant clusters and offer two options from among the word list for younger children to choose an appropriate beginning for each tongue twister. Invite older children to use the initial words and think up other endings to make tongue twisters.

See also: What's missing? (p55); Blend it (p78); Grab a crab (p84).

AGE RANGE 6–7

LEARNING OBJECTIVE
To discriminate between several consonant clusters at the ends of words.

CURRICULUM LINKS
NLS: Y1, T2, Word level 3.

Stamp!

What you need
Whiteboard; pen.

What to do
● Write the words *stamp*, *hand* and *fist* on the whiteboard, reading them to the children as you write. Say, *Look at the word 'stamp'. What sound do the last two letters 'mp' make in that word?* Repeat for the words *hand* and *fist*, inviting the children to tell you the sound made by the final two consonants in each word.

● Explain to the children that you would like them to listen for words that end with the same sounds as the three words on the board. Say, *Listen to the word 'band'. Does this word have the same sound at the end as the word 'stamp' or 'hand' or 'fist'?*

● When the children have given an answer, ask them to match the final sound in the word *lump* to the end sound of one of the three words on the board. Finally, check that they can hear that the word *nest* has the same sound at the end as the word *fist*.

● Now explain that you are going to read a list of words. Tell the children that if they hear an *mp* ending in the word, like in *stamp*, they must stamp on the floor. If they hear an *nd* ending, like in *hand*, they must wave their hands in their air. If they hear a word that ends with the sound *st*, like in *fist*, they should raise their fists in the air.

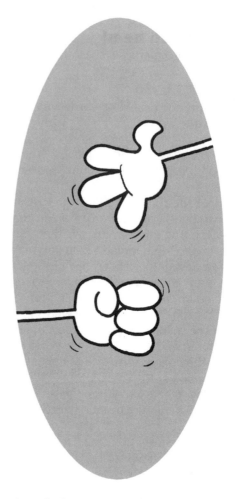

● Try the first three words from the first list below to make sure that the children understand what to do. Then use the following sequences of words:

band / fist / lump / bump / last / ramp / nest / mast / lend / strand
lamp / mist / best / mend / plump / vest / wind / land / stump / list
damp / hand / last / sand / chest / dump / stamp / bend / grand / rest.

Differentiation
For younger children, use only two of the final consonant clusters at a time and adjust the lists accordingly, emphasising the final sound in the words. For older and more able children, deliver the words fairly quickly and use two of the lists in a longer string.

See also: Blend the end (p57).

Match the middles

AGE RANGE 6–7

LEARNING OBJECTIVE
To distinguish the correct medial sound in given words and match these words to a second word with the same medial sound.

CURRICULUM LINKS
NLS: Y1, T2, Word level 1.

What you need
The 'Match the middles' photocopiable sheet on page 29; pencils.

What to do
● Make one photocopy of the 'Match the middles' sheet for each child.
● Show the sheets to the children and go through each of the pictures to ensure that the children know what these represent: bed; cup; cap; box; pig; cake; bike; sweet; cloud; coat; book; moon; sun; leaf; light; spoon; bone; grapes; foot; cat; log; pen; bin; mouse.
● Now ask the children to look at the first picture on the left hand side of the page and to tell you again what it is. Say, *Listen very carefully to the sound in the middle of the word 'bed'. Can you tell me what that sound is?*
● Encourage the children to look at all the pictures on the right side of the page and try to name one with the same middle sound as the word bed. Remind them that they are looking for something that has an *e* sound in the middle, just like *bed*.
● When the children have found the picture of the pen, say *That's right. The words 'bed' and 'pen' both have an 'e' sound in the middle. Write a number 1 in the little square by the pen to match the number 1 by the picture of the bed.*
● Now invite the children to work through the sheet, one picture at a time, reminding them to say the cue word to themselves and listen for the middle sound before they look for the picture with the matching middle sound. Make sure that they understand that they should then write a matching number in the corner of their chosen square.

Differentiation
With younger children, work through the sheet together, helping them to extract the middle sound from the cue words and offering a choice of two pictures from the right of the page from which to select the correct one. At the end of the activity, go through the cue words again, challenging older children to think of one more word each time which contains the same medial sound.

See also: Missing middle (p54).

AGE RANGE 6–7

LEARNING OBJECTIVE
To reinforce the role of silent *e* as a common spelling pattern for long vowel sounds.

CURRICULUM LINKS
NLS: Y2, T1, Word level 1.

Give me a clue

What you need
Whiteboard; pen; paper; pencils.

What to do
● Write the words *man* and *mane* on the board, inviting the children to listen to the final sounds of the two words as you say them. Point out that although the words look different at the end, they sound the same. Explain that it is the middle sound that has changed.
● Introduce the children to this rhyme to help them remember the role of silent *e*:

Whenever silent *e*'s around,
you'll never hear it make a sound.
When silent *e* is in the game,
it makes the vowel say its name.

● Write the following words on the board:
    slid   pan   cap   scrap   slim
    mat   twin   rip   slop   cub

● Explain to the children that you are going to give them a clue to one word in the list, and you would like them to write the word down. Say, *Find a word that is something you wear on your head.* Now tell the children that you would like them to change this word into something that they would wear round their shoulders, by adding a silent *e* to the word. Check their answers and work through another of the clues below, if necessary.
● Now read out more clues, inviting the children to use these to make new words from other words in the list:
1) Change something you use for cooking into the glass in a window.
2) Change a baby lion into a solid square shape.
3) Change a rug into a good friend.
4) Change a word meaning a tear into one meaning ready to eat.
5) Change a word meaning spill into ground which is not flat.
6) Change a word meaning not fat into a dirty ooze.
7) Change a person who looks exactly like his brother into a word meaning string.
8) Change a word meaning slipped into something you play on in the park.
9) Change a word meaning a small piece into a word meaning to rub against.

Differentiation
For younger children, write out the list of words in the same order that you intend to give the clues and limit the list to CVC words. Give other pairs of words to older and more able children and challenge them to create clues for one another:

hat / hate	cut / cute	win /wine	pip / pipe
fin / fine	tub / tube	cod / code	tap / tape
wag / wage	kit / kite	rag / rage	hug / huge

See also: Add / take away / switch (p58).

Phonic Fun!

AGE RANGE 6–7

LEARNING OBJECTIVE
To use a poem to explore two different spellings of the long *ee* sound.

CURRICULUM LINKS
NLS: Y2, T1, Word level 4.

Greedy Gilbert

What you need
Whiteboard or flipchart; two different coloured chalks or marker pens.

What to do
● Transcribe the poem 'Greedy Gilbert' below, onto a flipchart or whiteboard. Explain to the children that as you read the poem, you would like them to listen carefully for one sound that they will hear in lots of words in the poem.
● Read the poem, emphasising the long *ee* sounds slightly. When you have finished, invite the children to tell you which sound they heard in many of the words.

Gilbert was a greedy little beast,
who ate a thousand sweets for a feast.

After a huge meal cooked for his tea,
he would say, 'That was not enough for
 a flea.'

He'd stuff down his meat and gulp down
 his peas,
then grab some more, without saying please.

And, in deep sleep, Gilbert would dream
of beef pie and peanuts, peaches and cream.

© Jillian Harker

● Explain that the long *ee* sound can be spelled in several different ways, and that there are two different patterns used in the poem.
Write the two patterns at the top of the chart or board, using two different colours.
● Invite the children to look for words in the poem that contain either pattern. Ask them to underline words in the same colour that you used to write the relevant pattern.
● Explain that there is no rule to help us to choose the correct spelling pattern for the *ee* sound, but it can help us if we link several words together in our memory.
● Provide the children with the following sentences, inviting them to write the sentences on one side of a piece of paper and illustrate them on the reverse. Encourage the children to use different coloured pens for the *ee* and *ea* patterns:
    I dream of a meal of meat, peas, peaches and cream.
    The seal played on the beach by the sea.
    The wheels on the jeep slipped on the steep street.
    The queen is asleep in front of the TV screen.
    It is mean to cheat and steal.
● Use the pictures as cues, inviting the children to tell you the appropriate sentence and linked spelling pattern.

Differentiation
Omit the second part of the activity if you are working with younger children, and encourage them to list the words from the poem under the headings *ee words* and *ea words*. Provide more words which contain these patterns for older children, inviting them to construct further sentences as memory aids.

See also: Neat feet (p80).

 Phonic Fun!

AGE RANGE 6–8

LEARNING OBJECTIVE
To identify words in a poem which contain the long *ai* sound and categorise them according to their spelling pattern.

CURRICULUM LINKS
NLS: Y2, T2, Word level 1.

Raindrop race

What you need
The 'Raindrop race' photocopiable sheet on page 30; pencils; coloured pencils; three large sheets of paper, cut into raindrop shapes.

What to do
● Make one photocopy of the 'Raindrop race' sheet for each child.
● Tell the children that you are going to read them a poem that contains lots of words that have the same sound in them. Explain that you would like them to listen carefully and try to decide what that sound is. Read the poem *Raindrop race*, emphasising slightly the words with a long *ai* sound in them. Invite the children to suggest what the common sound was.
● Give each child a copy of the poem. Explain that when you read it for a second time, you would like them to underline every word in which they hear an *ai* sound. Read the poem again, but do not emphasise the words this time.
● Now invite the children to look at the words that they have underlined. Say, *All of those words had the same sound in them, but do they all have the same spelling pattern?*
● Show the children the three paper raindrop shapes. Write one of the spelling patterns *ae*, *ai* or *ay* on each drop. Explain that you would like the children to tell you which words they underlined and which drop you should write those words on, according to their spelling pattern. As you write down the words, encourage the children to circle them in three different colours on their sheet, according to their spelling pattern.
● When they have worked through the poem, explain that the *ai* sound can be spelled in many different ways, but that these three patterns are the most common.
● Count the words on each drop with the children to see which won the Raindrop race for the most words.

Differentiation
Before asking younger children to look for words in the poem, provide them with the three cue patterns to look for. Encourage older children to add to the lists other words they know which use the same spelling patterns for the *ai* sound.

See also: Frame it (p61).

AGE RANGE 6–8

LEARNING OBJECTIVE
To identify words which contain an '*r* pair' spelling pattern and to categorise these words into groups according to their spelling pattern.

CURRICULUM LINKS
NLS: Y2, T2, Word level 2.

Robber 'r'

What you need
The 'Robber 'r'' photocopiable sheet on page 31; pencils; whiteboard; pen

What to do
● Make one photocopy of the 'Robber 'r'' sheet for each child.
● Write the words *cat*, *cake* and *car* on a whiteboard, and ask the children to read the three words to you. Encourage them to tell you the sound that the letter *a* makes in *cat*, then the sound that the silent *e* helps it make in *cake*. Say, *Now listen to the word 'car'. Can you hear either the 'a' sound, like in 'cat', or the 'ai' sound, like in cake, in the word 'car'?*
● Explain that when the letter *r* follows a vowel, it robs the vowel of the two sounds that it usually makes. Say, *Robber 'r' makes the vowel 'a' join it to say a special sound.*
● Use other sets of words to illustrate how the *r* affects the sound of the other vowels:
  hen / here / her
  bit / bike / bird
  hot / hope / horn
  cut / cute / curl
● Give each child a copy of the 'Robber 'r'' photocopiable sheet. Explain that you would like them to look carefully at the groups of words and decide which words have a 'Robber 'r'' in them, stealing the sound of the vowel. Say that they must decide which of the robber's sacks to write the words in, depending on whether the pattern in each word is *ar*, *er*, *or*, *ir* or *ur*. Make sure that the children understand that not every word will be written in a sack – only those with an *r* pair in them.
● When the children have worked through the words and written them in the appropriate sacks, invite them to read their lists out.

Differentiation
With younger or less able children, work through the sheet with them, helping them to look for all the words with the *ar* pattern first, the *er* pattern next and so on. Challenge older and more able children to add other words to the sacks that they know have the same pattern.

See also: Pair it (p60); Lucky dip (p85).

AGE RANGE 6–8

LEARNING OBJECTIVE
To discriminate between two possible phonemes for the pattern *ea*, choosing the correct phoneme in a range of words.

CURRICULUM LINKS
NLS: Y2, T3, Word level 3.

Tea or bread?

What you need
Paper; pen; whiteboard; pencils.

What to do
● Make a photocopy master of the sentences below. Leave space between each sentence to allow for a small symbol to be drawn:
1) I enjoy a slice of bread with treacle for breakfast.
2) Weak tea is really very unpleasant.
3) They could not lift the heavy treasure chest.
4) It is not healthy to eat too much cream.
5) I must get some treatment for this dreadful headache.
6) The weather was very pleasant when we were at the beach.
7) My ideal way to relax would be sitting by a stream reading.
8) Did you see that flea leaping onto that leaf?
9) I am out of breath and sweating from trying to beat him in the race.
10) Are they ready to speak to the teacher now?

● Photocopy one sheet for each child.
● Draw a loaf of bread and a cup of tea on a whiteboard, and invite the children to tell you what these drawings are. Ask them whether the words *bread* and *tea* contain any sounds that are the same. Write the words beneath the drawings, underlining the *ea* pattern. Explain that the words do not share a common sound but they do have the same pattern, because *ea* can make more than one sound.
● Add the words *head* and *leaf*, asking the children whether the sound made by *ea* in these words is the same as in the word *tea* or the word *bread*.
● Give each child a photocopiable sheet. Ask the children to look through the sentences, underlining any word with an *ea* pattern. Say, *Now decide which of the sounds that pattern makes in each word. Draw a cup above a word if you think the 'ea' makes a sound like in 'tea', and a loaf of bread if you think the 'ea' makes a sound like in 'bread'.*
● Invite the children to read the sentences to you. Encourage them to think about whether the sentence makes sense and to change the symbol and sound if they have not read a word correctly.

Differentiation
Read the sentences for younger children. Ask them to add the symbols according to how you read the word, and then to read the sentence back to you. Challenge older and more able children to make a collection of other words in which the *ea* pattern makes the short sound as in *bread*.

AGE RANGE 7–8

LEARNING OBJECTIVE
To explore how many words can be built by using common spellings of the long vowel sounds with given word 'frames'.

CURRICULUM LINKS
NLS: Y3, T1, Word level 1.

Roll over

What you need
Paper; pencils; dice; six small stickers.

What to do
● Write one of the following patterns on each of the six stickers, and stick one to each side of the dice:

    ai   ee   ea   igh   oa   oo

● Invite four children to play a word game.
● Allocate each child one set of the following word frames:

r__d	gr__n	r__m	s__p
s__k	b__t	n__t	r__f
s__n	m__n	f__l	f__d
h__l	r__l	b__st	l__p

● Ask the children to write their four frames across the top of a piece of paper to form four headings.
● Explain to the children that they are going to take turns to roll the dice, and then decide whether they can use the pattern they throw in any one of their word frames to build a word. If they can, they then write the word they have made under the relevant heading. They can build only one word on each throw, but they are allowed to use any pattern again, with a different frame, if that pattern is thrown again on another turn.
● Explain that for the purposes of this game, the sound for the *oo* pattern is the sound that it makes in *boot*. Tell the children that the goal of the game is to see whether any of a player's frames can be used with all of the patterns to build real words. When players can build no further words, they drop out of the game. The winner is the person who has built the most words.
● Invite the children to begin the game, using the throw of a normal dice to decide the first player.

Differentiation
Check that younger children know the sound that each of the patterns on the dice makes. Provide adult support to help players decide whether certain patterns can be used correctly in given frames. Challenge older children to discover other word frames in which they can use at least two of the patterns to make words.

See also: Vowel teams (p82); Sound isn't everything (p83).

AGE RANGE 9–11

LEARNING OBJECTIVE
To explore words with the *–ough* pattern, linking its sounds to words with similar pattern / sound relationships.

CURRICULUM LINKS
NLS: Y4, T3, Word level 6.

One pattern, many sounds

What you need
Three differently coloured pieces of card, measuring approximately 8cm by 12cm, for each child; pencils; flipchart; three marker pens in the same colours as the card.

What to do
● Divide one sheet on the flipchart into three columns, heading each with the word *you*, *country* or *pound* in different colours. Ask the children to write one of these three words on each piece of card, matching the card colour to the colour that you used on the chart.
● Explain to the children that they are going to explore a spelling pattern which can make many different sounds. Say, *Which pattern can you see in all three words? Does it make the same sound in all of them?*
● Next, on a second sheet on the flipchart, list the following words:

soup	cousin	cloud	house	young
group	route	trouble	touch	shout
mouth	coupon	blouse	couple	youth

● Invite the children to sort these words into groups, according to the sound that the *ou* pattern makes, and to list them on the appropriate pieces of card under the cue words.
● Invite the children to help you compile a colour-coded master list on the chart. Explain that you are going to use the list to help you explore words that contain the pattern *ough*.
● Explain that in most words with the *ough* pattern the *gh* is silent and that it is the *ou* pattern which has many different sounds. Tell the children that there is only a small group of words where the *gh* makes an *f* sound.
● Say the following words one by one. Invite the children to listen carefully to the sound made by *ou* to decide in which column on the chart each word belongs: bough; through; rough; enough; tough; drought; thorough; borough.
● Add the words to the lists, circling the *gh* when it sounds *f* and pointing this out to the children. Encourage them to copy the words onto their appropriate cards.

Differentiation
Read the initial words with younger children, sorting them into groups together. Compile a list on the chart for them to copy onto their cards. Let older and more able children explore *ough* words such as *cough, trough, though, dough, ought, bought, fought, thought, sought, nought* and *brought*. Ask them to group the words according to whether the *ou* makes a short or long *o* sound or a sound like *aw*. Ask them to find the only two words in which the *gh* makes a sound.

Phonic Fun!

Licking lollies

 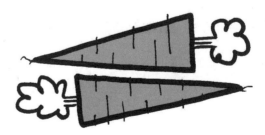

Which ending?

● Find the correct words to go with the pictures.

bed bet	mat mad	pot pod
cup cub	cap cab	sad sat
lit lid	nib nip	cod cot

Phonic Fun! BRIGHT IDEAS

Hunt the sound

● Tick the box to show whether the 'm' sound is at the beginning, middle or end of the word.

The pig in a wig

The pig in a wig

cannot do a jig.

He can't run or jog;

he is too fat a hog.

He sits in his sty

and looks at the sky.

'You must run,' said Dog.

'You must hop,' said Frog.

Pig did try to run,

but it was no fun.

He did try to hop,

but it was a flop.

'I am going to stop.

I just like to slop.

I can't run!' said Pig,

'and I don't give a fig!'

© Jillian Harker

Phonic Fun! **BRIGHT IDEAS**

Match the middles

● Find the words with the same middle sounds.

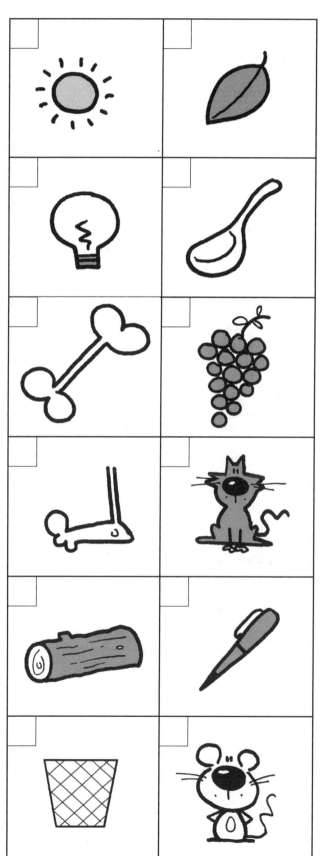

Raindrop race

● Listen to the poem, then underline any words you hear
that have an 'ai' sound in them.

I could hear the rain beating on the window

   pane,

and I couldn't wait 'til the sun came out again.

I hate it when I can't go out to play

So I wanted the rain to fade away.

But it just came trickling down that window

   pane –

one drop, another drop, rain rain rain!

And then I thought, 'I can still play!

I'll just have a game another way.

I'll see which raindrop wins first place

as they rush down the pane in a raindrop race.'

© Jillian Harker

Phonic Fun! **BRIGHT IDEAS**

Robber 'r'

● Find the words with Robber 'r' in them and
write them on the correct sacks.

fit	pack	luck	card	turn	peck	tart	pot
firm	park	lurk	dark	jerk	perk	burn	port
lard	corn	cart	term	cub	cod	bun	girl
lad	con	cat	pat	curb	cord	bid	cork
mark	fort	cad	part	kerb	curl	bird	first

ar

er

ir

or

ur

CHAPTER 2

Exploring and using rules

AGE RANGE 6–7

LEARNING OBJECTIVE
To explore which of two double letter patterns is the correct choice to complete given unfinished words in sentences.

CURRICULUM LINKS
NLS: Y1, T2, Word level 2.

Mixed doubles

What you need
A whiteboard or flipchart; marker pens.

What to do
● Transcribe the following onto the whiteboard or flipchart:

'll' or 'ss'?
I will mi__ you when you go.
The glass is fu__ of water.
Did you hear that snake hi__?
There is a mi__ on top of the hi__.

● Point out to the children that each of the sentences has one or more words with the ending missing. Explain that you would like them to help you to decide which of two endings, *ll* or *ss*, should be used to complete the sentence.
● Invite the children to tell you the sounds that the two endings make. Say, *Let's look at this word with an ending missing in the first sentence. It says, 'mi__'. If we add the 'll' ending, will that make a word?* Next, encourage the children to try the *ss* ending.
● Explain that although both endings will make real words, only one word will make sense in the sentence. Encourage the children to read the whole sentence, trying both of the word options before deciding which word makes sense. Then write in the correct ending.
● Work through each of the sentences in the same way, reminding the children that, although both endings will make a real word each time, only one choice will make sense.
● Now try a second exercise, inviting the children to choose between an *ll* and an *ff* ending for words in the following sentences:

'll' or 'ff'?
Can you pu__ the lid off?
A pu__ of smoke came from the fire.
He had a sti__ neck.
Is she sti__ asleep?
The steep hill made me hu__ and puff.

● Help the children to explore why these words have double letters at the end using the 'Listen and look' activity on page 33.

Differentiation
With younger children, sound out both word beginning and word ending for each alternative, inviting the children to blend these together to make the word choices. Read out the sentences for them. Invite older and more able children to decide which of the three endings – *ss*, *ff* or *ll* – could be used to complete these real words: spe__, ble__, cli__, stu__, che__, spi__.

Phonic Fun!

AGE RANGE 6–7

LEARNING OBJECTIVE
To understand that the vowel sound in a word can influence which of two spellings is used for the final sound 'l'.

CURRICULUM LINKS
NLS: Y2, T1, Word level 4.

Listen and look

What you need
A flipchart; marker pen; A4 paper; pencils.

What to do
● On the flipchart, draw a simple picture of an ear. Draw a row of three boxes underneath it. Give each child a piece of paper and a pencil and invite them to copy the boxes onto their paper.
● Explain that you are going to ask them to listen carefully to two words. If they think that the words begin with the same sound, they should put a tick in their first box. If not, they should put a cross. Give them the words *fell* and *feel*. Check that the children did a tick and do one yourself in the first box on the chart.
● Repeat the two words, this time inviting the children to listen to the final sound and to tick or cross the last box. Check their responses and tick the final box on the chart.
● Now focus on the middle sound, encouraging the children to listen again. Cross the middle box. Then say, *The words 'fell' and 'feel' have the same sounds at the beginning and end, but a different sound in the middle. Now let's see what they look like.*
● Draw a simple picture of an eye on the flipchart and three more boxes. Write *fell* and *feel* and discuss what the children see at the beginning, middle and end of the words, asking them to tick or cross their boxes again. Compare the sets of boxes, noticing that what you hear and what we see in the words is different. Invite the children to investigate some more pairs in the same way. For example: hell / heel; sell / seal; dell / deal.
● Finally, explain to the children that although the final sound of these pairs is exactly the same, it can be spelled with one or two *l*s, depending on the sound of the middle vowel. Tell the children that if they can hear the name of the vowel, they only need one letter *l*. If they can hear the short vowel sound, they need two letter *l*s at the end.

Differentiation
Emphasise the initial, final or medial phonemes to help younger children focus on given parts of the word. Give older and more able children words with a single *f* or *s* and a double *f* or *s* ending. Help them to compare the component sounds in these to extract the *flossy* rule: for words with one syllable and a single short vowel which end in *f*, *s* or *l* sounds, double the last letter.

AGE RANGE 8–9

LEARNING OBJECTIVE
To understand that the position of a particular sound *oy* in a word influences the choice of spelling for that sound.

CURRICULUM LINKS
NLS: Y4, T1, T2, T3, Word level 3.

Oy there!

What you need
A whiteboard or flipchart; marker pen; paper; pencils.

What to do
● Tell the children that you are going to read some sentences. Explain that you would like them to listen for two words in every sentence that contain the sound *oy* and to tell you what those two words are.
● Read the following sentences, pausing at the end of each for the children to name the *oy* sound words:

1) That boy makes a lot of noise.
2) I don't enjoy eating oysters.
3) You have a choice between boiled or baked potatoes.
4) It is annoying that the kettle takes so long to boil.
5) She is spoiling that toy by treating it so badly.

● As the children name the words, list them on the board or chart.
● Ask the children whether the sound *oy* is spelled in the same way in every word.
● Give each child a piece of paper and a pencil and invite them to write the headings *oy* and *oi* on their paper. Encourage the children to list the words from the sentences under the correct headings.
● Explain that the choice between the two spellings can be decided by listening to where the *oy* sound occurs in a word. Ask, *Are there any words in the 'oy' list where the 'oy' sound comes at the end of the word?* Tick the words as the children name them. Invite them to split the remaining two words into syllables. Ask, *Does the 'oy' sound come at the end of a syllable?*
● Now explore the *oi* words, encouraging the children to work out if the *oy* sound comes in the middle of the word or syllable in these examples.
● Remind the children that the *oy* pattern is used at the end of words or syllables, and invite them to use this knowledge to spell words such as *foil, employ, moist, toil, convoy* and *coy*.

Differentiation
For younger children, write the words on the board in different colours to help the children sort them into two lists. Show them how to gently rest their chin on the backs of their hands to help them feel syllables as they say a word. Provide older and more able children with a list of words such as *loiter, royal, loyal, avoid, voyage* and *exploit*. Ask them to explain the reason for the spelling of each word in terms of the rule they have discovered.

Bobo the clown

AGE RANGE 8–9

LEARNING OBJECTIVE
To use a poem to help pupils to deduce how to choose between the *ou* and *ow* patterns for the *ow* sound in words.

CURRICULUM LINKS
NLS: Y4, T3, Word level 5.

What you need
The 'Bobo the clown' photocopiable sheet on page 48; pencils.

What to do
● Make one copy of the photocopiable sheet for each child.
● Explain to the children that you are going to read them a poem in which many of the words contain the same sound. Ask them to listen carefully to try to work out what that sound is.
● Read the poem 'Bobo the clown'. When you have finished reading, invite the children to tell you the sound that occurred in many of the words. Explain that we use two different patterns to write this sound and ask whether anyone can suggest what these patterns might be. Use the cue words *out* and *down* to help the children, if necessary. Explain that you are going to try to find out how they might choose which pattern to use if they were unsure how to spell a particular word.
● Give each child a copy of the poem. Explain that they should work through each verse, underlining any word with an *ow* sound. Point out the headings at the end of the poem, asking the children to write each of the underlined words under one of the headings. Suggest that they check each word against each heading in turn, working from left to right, to help them decide in which list the word belongs.

● When the children have completed their lists, encourage them to check whether all the words in the list share a common spelling pattern for the *ow* sound. Invite them to suggest how checking a word against these headings could help them to make the correct choice of spelling for the *ow* sound. If necessary, help them to reach the conclusion that we use the *ow* pattern if the *ow* sound comes at the end of a word or syllable, or if it is followed by *n* or *l* to make a word. Otherwise we use the *ou* pattern.
● Challenge the children to check whether the words *foul*, *crowd* and *browse* fit the rule or are exceptions.

Differentiation
Work through the poem a line at a time with younger children, and discuss under which heading each underlined word should be listed. Encourage older children to generate other words which contain an *ow* sound to add to each of the lists.

See also: How does it sound? (p64).

AGE RANGE 8–9

LEARNING OBJECTIVE
To categorise words found in a wordsearch to formulate a rule relating to the choice of the *aw* or *au* patterns for the *aw* sound.

CURRICULUM LINKS
NLS: Y4, T3, Word level 5.

Find the flaw

What you need
The 'Find the flaw' photocopiable sheet on page 49; pencils.

What to do
● Make one copy of the photocopiable sheet for each child.
● Explain to the children that they are going to look for 17 words in the wordsearch which contain the sound *aw*. Tell them that they will find this sound spelled in two different ways, either with an *aw* pattern or with an *au* pattern. (Wordsearch answers: *lawn, hawk, sauce, shawl, yawn, tawny, dawn, law, laundry, awful, saw, paw, naughty, crawl, dawdle, fault, raw.*)
● When the children have completed the wordsearch, explain that for the second part of the task you would like them to list the words that they have found under certain headings. Take them through the headings beneath the wordsearch, ensuring that they understand the importance of listening to where the *aw* sound occurs in the word. Remind them of what is meant by a syllable. Use the word *awful* as an example of a word in which the *aw* sound comes at the end of a syllable.
● When they have listed all the words, invite the children to comment on the spelling patterns used in each list. Discuss whether there is a word in the final list that stands out from the rest. (Answer is *hawk*.)
● Encourage the children to use the headings to help them think of some questions they could ask themselves when trying to spell a word with an *aw* sound, that would help them to choose the correct spelling pattern. Which word would be an exception?
● Finally, invite the children to comment on any similarities with a rule encountered in the 'Bobo the clown' activity on page 35.

Differentiation
With younger children, encourage a systematic approach to the wordsearch, scanning rows first and then columns, looking for either of the two patterns. Help the children to sort all the words that fit under the first heading before moving to the next, emphasising the sequence of questions which would produce the correct choice of spelling pattern. Let older and more able children discover the two spelling patterns for themselves at the beginning of the activity, and challenge them to discover any other exceptions to the rule, giving clues such as *maul* and *haul* if necessary.

Phonic Fun! **BRIGHT IDEAS**

AGE RANGE 8–9

LEARNING OBJECTIVE
To use a poem to explore the occurrence of the letter pattern *ck* at the end of words and to deduce when this pattern is used to spell the *k* sound.

CURRICULUM LINKS
NLS: Y4, T3, Word level 5.

Jack's old truck

What you need
The 'Jack's old truck' photocopiable sheet on page 50; coloured pencils or highlighters; flipchart; marker pen.

What to do
● Make one copy of the photocopiable sheet for each child.
● Explain to the children that the poem contains lots of words which all have a *k* sound, spelt with a *ck* pattern. Invite them to read through the poem and to underline each example of such words that they can find.
● When the children have worked through the poem, underlining the words, ask them to list those words under the five headings below the poem, according to whether the spelling pattern in the word is *ack, eck, ick, ock* or *uck*.
● Now write the following words on the flipchart: *cake, like, soak, duke*. Invite the children to read the words, listening carefully to the final sound. Do these words end with the same sound as words from the poem, such as *muck* and *black*? Is this sound written in the same way in both sets of words?
● Add another set of words to the chart: *bank, desk, milk, plonk, sulk*. Invite the children to tell you whether these end in the same sound as the other two sets. Is the *k* sound spelled the same as the words in the poem or those on the flipchart?
● Explain to the children that we only ever use the *ck* pattern when the *k* sound immediately follows a short vowel sound, that is when we hear *ack, eck, ick, ock* or *uck*. At other times we spell the final *k* sound with a *k* alone.
● Follow up this activity with 'Now you c it' on page 38.

Differentiation
Read the poem to younger children, asking them to underline the words with a *ck* pattern as you read. Help them to decide under which headings the words should be listed. Invite older and more able children to add as many words as possible that use the same pattern to each of the word lists and to check that the rule works in these words.

AGE RANGE 8–9

LEARNING OBJECTIVE
To choose correctly between two possible spellings of a word, applying knowledge of the *ck* rule.

CURRICULUM LINKS
NLS: Y5, T3, Word level 3.

Now you c it

What you need
The 'Now you c it' photocopiable sheet on page 51; pencils, whiteboard; marker pen.

What to do
● Make one copy of the 'Now you c it' photocopiable sheet for each child.
● Remind the children that a *k* sound at the end of a word can be spelled in different ways. Write the words *back*, *bake* and *bank* on the whiteboard, underlining the *ck* pattern in the first word and the *k* in the other two.
● Remind the children that the *ck* ending is only used when a *k* sound comes immediately after a short vowel sound like in *back*. We have to hear *ack*, *eck*, *ick*, *ock* or *uck* words to use the *ck* ending.
● We use a *k* on its own in words where the *k* sound follows long vowels, like in *bake* (*ai*, *ee*, *ie*, *oa* or *oo* words). The letter *k* is also used alone when another letter comes between a short vowel and the *k* sound, like in *bank*. Write the sample words on the board as you explain this.
● Invite the children to look at the photocopiable sheet. Explain that you would like them to choose between the two words beneath the pictures and circle the word that is the correct spelling for the picture.
● After this they should read the short passage at the bottom of the page and fill in the gaps with either *ck* or *k* to complete the spelling of the unfinished words correctly.

Differentiation
With younger children, focus only on the picture exercise. Encourage the children to say the word that goes with each picture. Each time ask, *Can you hear 'ack', 'eck', 'ick', 'ock' or 'uck' in that word? Only choose the 'ck' spelling if you can hear one of those sound patterns.* Invite older and more able children to explain their choices of spelling, showing knowledge of the rule by saying, for example, *I didn't choose that spelling because there is already another letter between the short vowel and the letter 'k'.*

See also: Three in one (p53); Families (p73).

To the rescue

AGE RANGE 9–11

LEARNING OBJECTIVE
To understand the rule that governs the choice between *ch* and *tch* in spelling the *ch* sound at the end of words.

CURRICULUM LINKS
NLS: Y5, T2, Word level 4.

What you need
A flipchart; marker pen; overhead projector and acetate.

What to do
● Make an acetate master showing the spelling rule rhymes below.
● Write the following words on the flipchart: *match, fetch, branch, poach, couch, perch.*
● Point out the two patterns which spell the *ch* sound to the children, explaining that there are rules which can help them to make the correct choice between *ch* and *tch* in such words.
● Read the following rules, one at a time:

Rule 1
a, e, i, o, u are short vowel sounds,
but these vowels need protection when *ch* is around.
So along comes their friend, the kind letter *t*
and says, 'I'll stand by you. Just depend on me.'
● Explain that the letter *t* is there to protect the short vowel from *ch* in the words *match* and *fetch*.

Rule 2
Letters *l* and *n* say, 'Hey! We help out, too.
When we are around, those short vowels don't need you!'
● Explain that the letter *n* is already protecting the short vowel from *ch* in the word *branch*.

Rule 3
The long vowels – that's the ones that say their name,
agree, 'We don't need *t* either. For us, it's the same.'
● Explain that the letters *oa* in *poach* make a long sound and this does not need protecting from *ch*.

Rule 4
Vowel pairs like *ou* say, 'We've already got a friend.
We're happy without *t*, just with *ch* at the end.'
● Explain that pairs of vowels, as in *couch*, do not need the extra letter either.

Rule 5
'We're the same', the *r* pair vowels begin to shout.
'It's just those short vowels on their own that are the odd ones out!'
● Explain that a vowel followed by an *r* (for example, in *perch*) does not need the extra *t*.
● Ask the children to number each of the words below to link it to the appropriate rhyming rule.

batch	filch	clutch
bunch	hitch	pitch
reach	march	lurch
stretch	pouch	grouch
porch	pinch	beach

● Explain that there are four common exceptions: *rich, which, much* and *such.*

Differentiation
With younger children, emphasise that the *t* only occurs in words with the sound patterns *atch, etch, itch, otch,* or *utch*. Work through the word list together. Challenge older or more able children to find one more word to illustrate each rhyme.

AGE RANGE 9–11

LEARNING OBJECTIVE
To understand the rule for choosing between the *–dge* and *–ge* spelling patterns.

CURRICULUM LINKS
NLS: Y5, T2, Word level 4.

Judge for yourself

What you need
A flipchart; marker pen; coloured pencils; pencils.

What to do
● Make a master of the following story and copy it for each child:

I was pulling my sledge along in the snow the other day, when a huge badger charged out of the hedge and barged straight into me. I fell onto the sledge, which plunged at once down the hill. It headed for the grass verge at the bottom, and I could see that the danger was that it would forge its way over the edge of the verge and into the road. I might be lucky and dodge the traffic, or I might need urgent hospital treatment. In fact, there was a large stone lodged in the grass and the sledge wedged itself on this. I was in a rage with that badger. It should be locked up in a cage! The strange thing was that the badger seemed to notice nothing and trudged on through the snow without looking back.

● Invite the children to read the story, underlining the words with a *–dge* pattern in one colour and those with a *–ge* pattern in another.
● Encourage them to list all of the *–dge* words. Explain that only the short vowels need an extra letter between them and *–ge*.
● Now ask the children to look at other underlined words from the passage. Why do the words *huge*, *rage*, *cage*, *strange* and *danger* not need the letter *d*? Encourage them to comment on the vowel sounds.
● Next, ask the children to find words with a vowel followed by *r*. Why do these not need the extra letter?
● Focus on the word *plunge*. Encourage the children to use their knowledge from the 'To the rescue' activity on page 39, if appropriate, to explain the absence of a letter *d*. Otherwise, point out that there is already a letter *n* between the short vowel and the *–ge*.

Differentiation
Read the story to younger children, asking them to underline all the words in which they hear a *j* sound. List the *–dge* words, explaining that this spelling pattern is only used when we hear *adge*, *edge*, *idge*, *odge* or *udge* in a word. Read the *–ge* words, asking whether any of those sounds can be heard. Challenge older and more able children to list ten more words with a *–dge* spelling pattern.

Phonic Fun!

Keep your distance

AGE RANGE 9–11

LEARNING OBJECTIVE
To understand how the difference in vowel sounds impacts on the spelling of words with an –*le* ending.

CURRICULUM LINKS
NLS: Y5, T1, T2, T3, Word level 3; Y6, T1, T2, T3, Word level 3.

What you need
An opaque bag; apple; pebble; slip of paper; pen; bottle; tub of bubble soap; whiteboard or flipchart; marker pens.

What to do
● Write a simple riddle on the slip of paper and place this in the bag together with the apple, pebble, bottle and bubble soap.

● In turn, invite the children to put a hand into the bag, grasp an item, guess what it is and remove it to check. Ask what is written on the paper. List the following words on the board as the children name the objects, arranged in vowel order: *apple, pebble, riddle, bottle, bubble.*

● Invite the children to suggest common features in the words, such as the –*le* ending and the double letters.

● Now give some clues to another set of words:

We sit at this to eat (*table*)
The pointed roof of a church (*steeple*)
The name of a book (*title*)
To stare in an unpleasant way (*ogle*)
A brass instrument (*bugle*)

● Invite the children to compare both sets of words, drawing their attention to the single consonants before the –*le* ending. Ask whether they can think of any difference between the first and second set of words which may explain why one set has a double letter and the other does not? The clue is in the vowel sounds.

● Discuss the fact that there must be two consonants between a short vowel and the ending –*le*, explaining that this means that we may have to double a letter to ensure this.

● Check this rule by exploring more words:
middle (*short vowel, double letter needed*)
bumble (*short vowel, but two consonants already there*)
trifle (*long vowel, double consonant not needed*)
purple (*'r pair', two consonants already there*)

● Invite the children to suggest other words to check the rule.

Differentiation
Before starting work, remind younger children of the difference between the short and long vowel sounds. Target questions carefully, to guide the children to see similarities and differences, saying, for example, *Do these words all have the same ending? Do they all have a double letter before the '–le'?* and so on.

Invite older children to explore the words *double* and *trouble*. What would the vowel sound lead us to expect in the spelling? Has spelling the short vowel sound with two letters affected this?

See also: Double or quits (p86).

Which way round?

AGE RANGE 9–10

LEARNING OBJECTIVE
To check whether a given spelling rule works for the majority of words and to decide which words are exceptions.

CURRICULUM LINKS
NLS: Y5, T3, Word level 5.

What you need
Pencils; paper; flipchart or whiteboard; marker pens.

What to do
● Transcribe the following rhyme onto a flipchart or a whiteboard:

i before *e*, *e* before *i*? Which way round?
All you have to do is listen for the sound.
If you're sure the sound you want is *ee*,
write *i* before *e*, except after *c*.
If the sound you need is *ai* or *igh*,
then write the *e* first, followed by *i*.

● Read the rhyme to the children. Explain that the spelling patterns *ie* and *ei* cause a lot of confusion, but that the rhyme above will help them to understand in which order they should use these letters.
● Write the word *piece* on the chart. Point out that the sound in the middle of this word is *ee* and so the rule in the third and fourth lines of the rhyme apply.
● Compare this with the word *receive*, explaining that although the *ee* sound is the same, it follows immediately after a letter *c*, so the spelling order is reversed.
● Finally, add the word *vein* to the chart, emphasising the medial *ai* sound, and referring to the final two lines of the rhyme.
● Now explain that you would like the children to check whether certain words fit this rule, and if there are any exceptions. Ask them to divide their paper into four columns with the headings:
    Sound 'ee', not after 'c'
    Sound 'ee', after 'c'
    Sound 'ai' or 'igh'
    Exception
● Write the following words on the chart:

ceiling	chief	rein	neigh	seize
field	niece	deceive	perceive	protein
conceit	height	believe	shield	reign
freight	relief	conceive	veil	thief

● Invite the children to categorise the words under the headings, using the rhyme as a reminder.

Differentiation
Work through the words together with younger children, reading them to the children and using cue questions, such as, *Did you hear an 'ee' sound?* Give the words in category order, dealing with all the words for the first column, then for the second, and so on.

For older and more able children, do not provide headings, but encourage them to sort the words into groups according to sound and pattern and to suggest headings themselves.

Phonic Fun!

AGE RANGE 9–11

LEARNING OBJECTIVE
To locate words containing the letter *c* in a set of sentences, distinguish between the sounds *c* makes in those words and decide which vowels might influence this sound.

CURRICULUM LINKS
NLS: Y5, T2, Word level 4.

Softies

What you need
Flipchart or whiteboard; marker pen; paper; pencils.

What to do
● Transcribe the following sentences onto a flipchart or whiteboard:

Slice through the centre of the cake.
Take a short cut to the city on your cycle.
The cat tipped the cup over twice.
You must collect the parcel from the post office.
Did you notice the candles in the cellar?

● Invite the children to locate three words in each sentence which contain the letter *c*. Underline the words as they suggest them. Ask, *Does the letter 'c' make the same sound in all of those words? If not, how many different sounds does it make?*
● Give each child a sheet of paper and a pencil, and ask them to write the headings *'k' sound* and *'s' sound*. Encourage the children to list the words under these two headings.
● When they have done this, explain that the sound of the letter *c* is influenced by the letter that follows it. Encourage the children to examine their lists and suggest which vowels soften the sound of *c* to an *s* sound.
● Now present the children with a second set of sentences:

The huge giant stamped down the garden path.
The goat did a lot of damage when it went on the
 rampage.
You need lots of energy to go to the gym every day.
George was chewing gum in the geography lesson.
I got a pen and wrote a message on the blank page.

● Invite them to explore all of the words containing a letter *g* in the same way as they have just done with *c*. Can they find any similarities when *g* is followed by certain vowels?
● Finally, ask the children to examine the words containing a *g* in this sentence:

Get a gift and give it to the girl.

● Do these words fit the rule they have just worked out?

Differentiation
For younger children, underline the soft *c* and hard *c* words in different colours. Explain how the following vowel changes the sound. Invite them to colour code the letter *g* words in the same way, according to the following vowel. Read the sentences together. Ask older and more able children to make a collection of as many soft *c* and *g* words as they can.

AGE RANGE 9–11

LEARNING OBJECTIVE
To be able to demonstrate understanding of the suffixing rule with silent *e* words.

CURRICULUM LINKS
NLS: Y5, T3, Word level 5.

Replace or leave?

What you need
Sheets of A4 card; scissors; pens.

What to do
● List the following words down the left-hand side of a sheet of A4 card:
make   hope   take   smile   ride   drive
● Cut slits in the right-hand side of the card, level with the bottom of each word. Fold the resulting strips of card, so that the end of each strip covers the silent *e* of one word. Write *ing* on the strip to replace the *e*. Now open out the strips to reveal the original words (see diagram below).
● Make a second card, using the words:
lone   tune   hope   base   tire   nice
● This time, fold the strips over less so that the silent *e* is left visible. Write the suffixes –*ly*, –*ful*, –*less*, –*ment*, –*some* and –*ness* on the strips, following directly on from the silent *e* of each word (see diagram below).
● Show the children the first card. Explain that in English, we often add a letter, or a group of letters, to the end of a word. These endings are called suffixes and there are rules about adding suffixes to silent *e* words.
● Flip over the top strip of card. Tell the children that when we add –*ing* to a silent *e* word, the suffix replaces the letter *e*. As you flip over each strip, say, for example, *Hope – ing*. Explain that we must replace the *e* because to leave it would mean that vowel digraphs would be formed and an unwanted sound created. Say that we replace the *e* with any suffix beginning with a vowel.
● Now use the second card to demonstrate that the *e* is left in place when adding any consonant suffix.
● Next, invite the children to construct their own A4 card to show what would happen when the following words and suffixes are combined:
hope + ing
shake + y
safe + ly
rude + ness
mine + er
tire + less
time + ing
hate + ful
● Make it clear that they will need to fold back each strip to either cover the silent *e* or not, as appropriate.

Differentiation
Help younger children to make their own cards and order the words so that the vowel suffixes are grouped at the top of the card. Encourage older and more able children to make a second card, with their own choice of silent *e* words and the same set of suffixes.

See also: Drop it (p87).

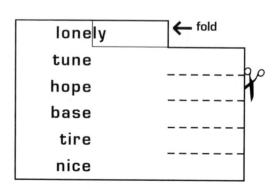

Phonic Fun!   **BRIGHT IDEAS**

AGE RANGE 9–10

LEARNING OBJECTIVE
To understand that English words cannot end with a
letter *i* and so use *y*, and that this final *y* reverts to *i*
when a suffix is added.

CURRICULUM LINKS
NLS: Y5, T3, Word level 5.

Why?

What you need
A flipchart or whiteboard; marker pens.

What to do
● Transcribe the following poem onto the flipchart:

Frog, my friend, I should not pry,
but, tell me, did you spy that fly
that just went buzzing by?

My froggy friend, please do not cry!
That big fat fly was very spry
and that's the only reason why
you did not catch that juicy fly.

It really cannot be denied –
that juicy fly, indeed, I spied
To catch that fly I really tried,
but failed – and that is why I cried.

© Jillian Harker

● Read the first two verses to the children.
● Explain that we use a *y* at the end of many words to write an *igh* sound, because
English words cannot end with an *i*. Underline the final letter *y* in appropriate words.
(Although the sound is different, final *y* in words such as *juicy* occurs for the same
reason.)
● Encourage the children to listen for the *igh* sounds now in the last verse,
remembering that there cannot be an *i* at the end of an English word.
● Read the final verse, inviting the children to tell you which words contained an *igh*
sound. As they do so, underline the letter *i*. Notice that the *y* spelling has disappeared
from these words and there is an *i* instead. Can they think of a reason for this? Prompt
the children, if necessary, to think about whether the *igh* sound is now at the end of
the words.
● Explain that, in adding a suffix to a word ending in *y*, that letter is no longer at the
end, and can revert to a letter *i*. Add that this is not the case when adding *–ing* because
this would produce a double letter *i*.

Differentiation
For younger children write the base words, such as *deny* and *spy* from the final verse.
Ask the children where the *y* comes in the word, and then add the *–ed* ending so that
they can see this has changed the position of the *y*. Change it to *i*. Challenge older and
more able children to think of words that end in an *i* (taxi, ski, spaghetti) and ask why
this is so. (They are not English words in origin.)

See also: Drop it (p87).

AGE RANGE 10–11

LEARNING OBJECTIVE
To understand when to double the final letter of a word before adding –ing.

CURRICULUM LINKS
NLS: Y6, T1, T2, T3, Word level 3.

Find the rule

What you need
Flipchart or whiteboard; marker pens; paper; pencils.

What to do
● Divide the flipchart into four columns. Fill these in as follows to build up the lists given below.
● Write the words in the first column and invite the children to read them. Say, *Now I'm going to write those same words in a second column with 'ing' added.*
● Fill in the second column, asking the children whether they notice anything that these words have in common. If necessary, draw their attention to the double letters.
● Now complete the third column and invite the children to read the words. Say, *Next, I'm going to write those same words with 'ing' added.*
● Fill in the fourth column, asking the children whether these words have a double letter before *ing*.

hop	hopping	read	reading
nod	nodding	soak	soaking
flap	flapping	land	landing
strum	strumming	rest	resting
beg	begging	sleep	sleeping

● Explain to the children that all the words in the first column have three things in common, which means we have to double the last letter when we add *ing*. Invite them to complete the following statements about the first set of words:
These words all have _____ syllable.
These words all have _____ short vowel.
These words all have _____ final consonant.
● Explain that this 1-1-1 rule tells us when we need to double the last letter when adding vowel suffixes, including *ing*. Now work through each word in the third column, checking whether it has one syllable, one short vowel and one final consonant. Explain that if any one of these characteristics is missing, the doubling rule does not apply.
● Invite the children to copy the following passage, adding *ing* to the words indicated, and doubling where necessary:

Keep___ to the rules when spell___ can be helpful. Stop____ yourself add___ a double letter when it is not needed means you can go skip____ off at break. When others are sit____, put____ right their spell___ mistakes, you can be jump__ or hop___ round the playground, kick___ a ball.

● Follow with the 'Double or not?' on page 47.

Differentiation
Carry out the cloze exercise as a group with younger children. With each word, ask the children whether it has one syllable, one vowel and one consonant at the end, emphasising that only then should they double the final letter. Encourage older and more able children to suggest common characteristics for the words in the first column before giving the statements for them to complete.

See also: Drop it (p87).

AGE RANGE 10–11

LEARNING OBJECTIVE
To be able to correctly decide whether or not to double the final letter in a word before adding a suffix.

CURRICULUM LINKS
NLS: Y6, T1, T2, T3, Word level 3.

Double or not?

What you need
The 'Double or not?' photocopiable sheet on page 52; pencils.

What to do
● This activity is best used to follow up the previous activity 'Find the rule' on page 46.
● Make one copy of the photocopiable sheet for each child.
● Explain to the children that their task is to find their way from the top left corner of the grid to the bottom right corner. Explain that there is only one correct way through and they will need to spell words and write them down as they go.
● Invite the children to look at the word *hit*. Tell them that they have to decide whether or not you double the last letter when they add *ing* to the word *hit*. Ask them to write down how they think the word *hitting* should be spelled. If they doubled the letter *t*, then they move on to the 'yes' square and follow the arrow to the next word. Again, they must decide whether to double or not when adding *ing*.
● Explain to the children that they should have written down 15 words if they have made their way through the grid correctly, and that you will check their spelling of these words. The correct route through the grid and correct answers are as follows:
hitting; *stopping*; *standing*; *getting*; *humming*; *reading*; *ripping*; *helping*; *melting*; *budding*; *letting*; *weeding*; *gripping*; *pumping*; *tapping*.

Differentiation
Work through the grid with younger children. Give frequent reminders that they only double a letter before adding *ing* when the word fits the 1-1-1 rule (see 'Find the rule' on page 46). Challenge older and more able children to create a grid of their own.

See also: Drop it (p87).

Bobo the clown

Now Bobo the clown is coming to town,
I think you had better be quick and duck down.
Don't stop to sniff at Bobo's bright flower,
or that rowdy clown will give you a shower.

'Bow down!' people shout, when Bobo's about.
'You need to stay down, you need to look out!'
He comes from behind and you won't hear a
sound.
You have to take care when Bobo's around.

You cannot hide inside your house.
He creeps up on you as quiet as a mouse.
Before you have the time to shout,
He'll spray you with his water spout.

Bobo won't care if he sees you frown.
Bobo won't care if he hears you howl.
If you don't keep down when Bobo's in town,
Then you will need a very large towel.

Don't let him pounce, just keep a look out.
If you see him around, then give me a shout.

© Jillian Harker

● Find all of the words with an 'ow' sound and write them under the correct heading.

'ow' sound comes at the end of a word or end of a syllable	'ow' sound comes in the middle of a syllable followed by 'n' or 'l'	Does not fit the first two headings
_____	_____	_____
_____	_____	_____
_____	_____	_____
_____	_____	_____
_____	_____	_____
_____	_____	_____
_____	_____	_____

Phonic Fun!   **BRIGHT IDEAS**

Find the flaw

● Find all the words with an 'aw' sound, spelt with an 'aw' or an 'au' pattern.

l	a	w	n	h	a	w	k	f
a	w	s	a	u	c	e	l	a
u	f	a	u	b	r	d	d	u
n	u	w	g	u	a	s	a	l
d	l	s	h	a	w	l	w	t
r	d	a	t	k	l	h	d	f
y	i	p	y	a	w	n	l	r
o	t	a	w	n	y	t	e	a
d	a	w	n	o	j	l	a	w

● Now list the words you have found in the correct columns.

'aw' sound comes at the end of a word or end of a syllable	'aw' sound comes in the middle of a syllable followed by 'n' or 'l' to complete the word	Does not fit the first two headings
_____	_____	_____
_____	_____	_____
_____	_____	_____
_____	_____	_____
_____	_____	_____
_____	_____	_____

● Write the word from the final column which is the odd one out: _____

Jack's old truck

● Read the poem and underline all the words which use a 'ck' pattern.

One day on a track Jack's very old truck
got stuck in some very tacky black muck.
He gave it a slap and he gave it a smack,
but it wouldn't go forwards and wouldn't go back.

'I'll be quick,' said Jack, 'and I'll give it a kick.
If I'm lucky, a kick might just do the trick.'
But poor Jack soon found he could not kick his truck,
His boots were both stuck in the black tacky muck.

Jack looked at the muck and the truck and took stock
'I'll just have to take off one boot and one sock.'
He pulled at his boot and down he fell – smack!
So there lay poor Jack, in the muck, on his back.

There was muck in his hair and muck down his neck.
Jack lay on the deck and grumbled, 'Oh heck!
That trick didn't work. I'm sick of this muck,
but, most of all, I'm really sick of my truck!'

© Jillian Harker

● List the words you underlined under the correct heading, matching the spelling pattern. Write each word only once.

–ack	–eck	–ick	–ock	–uck
_____	_____	_____	_____	_____
_____	_____	_____	_____	_____
_____	_____	_____	_____	_____
_____	_____	_____	_____	_____
_____	_____	_____	_____	_____

Now you c it

● Circle the correct spelling for each picture.

soak / sock	sink / sick	snack / snake
duck / duke	lick / like	peek / peck
deck / desk	tank / tack	tack / take

● Fill in the gaps with a 'ck' or 'k' pattern.

My friend had a ti____et sti____ing out of his ja____et po____et. 'Is that what I think____ it is?' I as____ed him.
'Oh he____,' he said, with a wi____ed grin. 'Just my stin____ing lu____ that you would see the ti____et. This is tri____y. I thought that I had tu____ed it right into my po____et.'
'I ta____e it that I wasn't intended to know,' I said, and I shoo____ my head. 'You know how much I like cri____et. I could have come too.'
'Wa____e up,' my friend said. 'Can't you see it's a ti____et for two. I was going to ta____e you with me. You can buy a pa____et of sweets in the shop for a sna____. I li____e those sti____y red ones.'

Double or not?

● Make your way through the grid, beginning in the top left corner and finishing in the bottom right corner.

● Decide whether you must double the last letter when adding 'ing' to each word you pass. Write down your chosen spelling below the grid. Then follow the 'yes' arrow if you have doubled, and the 'no' arrow' if you have not, to move to the next word.

hit	yes →	stop	no →	crash	no →	rest	no ↓
no ↓		yes ↓		yes →	lap	yes →	
get	← no	stand	yes ↓		yes →	melt	no ↓
yes ↓			rip	yes →	help	no ↑	bud
hum	yes →	read	no ↑			yes ↓	let	← yes
no ↓		yes ↓		no ↓	weed		
run	no ↓	add		grip	yes ↓		
	stamp	yes ↓		no ↓	pump	no →	tap
	← no		← yes	crush	no →		**yes**

Answers

1 _____	6 _____	11 _____
2 _____	7 _____	12 _____
3 _____	8 _____	13 _____
4 _____	9 _____	14 _____
5 _____	10 _____	15 _____

Phonic Fun! **BRIGHT IDEAS**

CHAPTER 3

Using what you know

AGE RANGE 5–7

LEARNING OBJECTIVE
To read a set of simple words, discover rhyming patterns in those words and to track the alphabet in the correct order.

CURRICULUM LINKS
NLS: Y1, T1, World levels 1, 2, and 5.

Three in one

What you need
The 'Three in one' photocopiable sheet on page 69; pencils.

What to do
● Make one copy of the photocopiable sheet for each child.
● Invite the children to look at the list of words at the top of the sheet. Move round the group, asking individual children to read one or more of the words on the sheet, working along the rows, until the full set has been read.
● Now say, *If we look along the first line of words, we will find a word that rhymes with 'dad'. Can you see what it is?* When the children have answered, ask them whether the words *dad* and *mad* have the same sound at the beginning or at the end. Discuss the fact that they have the same two letters at the end as well.
● Next, point out the ending patterns in the middle of the sheet. Explain to the children that you would like them to now find three words in the word list that end with each of the patterns and write them under the appropriate pattern. Remind them that these words will rhyme.
● Now ask the children to look at the first word in the word list. Can they see a letter *a* in that word? Ask them to underline it.
● Explain that they must find a letter *b* in the second word, a letter *c* in the third word, and so on, underlining these letters each time, until they have found the whole alphabet.

Differentiation
Help younger children to sound out the words for reading and work as a group to find the rhyming patterns. Provide an alphabet line to act as a prompt for the children, to help them to find the letters in the correct order. Invite older and more able children to make lists of other words that contain the rhyme patterns and to talk about whether it is easier to create a longer list for any particular pattern.

AGE RANGE 5–7

LEARNING OBJECTIVE
To choose the correct letter from two options
to spell the middle sound in simple words.

CURRICULUM LINKS
NLS: Y1, T1, Word level 4.

Missing middle

What you need
The 'Missing middle' photocopiable sheet on page 70; pencils.

What to do
● Make one copy of the 'Missing middle' photocopiable sheet for each child.
● Invite the children to look at the first picture on the sheet and to tell you what it is.
Ask them to tell you the first sound in the word and what letter we would use to write
that sound. Then ask the children to give you the final sound in the word and the letter
we would use to write that sound.
● Point out to the children that the first and last letter of the word have been written
underneath the picture.
● Explain that they need one more letter to complete the word, and it's the letter that
writes the middle sound.
● Encourage them to look at the two possible letters that have been written for the
middle of the word: *a* and *o*.
● Invite the children to tell you the medial sound from the word and then ask whether
they would use the letter *a* or the letter *o* to write that middle sound? They can try
saying the word with the two different letters and hear the difference in the sounds.
● Encourage the children to circle the correct answer and then to write the word out in
full underneath the picture.
● Invite the children to work through the rest of the sheet in this way, circling the
correct letter to write the middle sound of each word, and then writing the word out in
full underneath.

Differentiation
Help younger children to segment each word into three separate sounds before looking
at the letters. Emphasise the middle sound to help them make the correct choice of
letter. Provide older and more able children with other examples of initial and final
letters, (r–t, b–g, m–p, d–n, s–p) and challenge them to find two options for a middle
letter, both of which would write a real word.

Phonic Fun!

AGE RANGE 6–7

LEARNING OBJECTIVE
To correctly identify which letter has been omitted from words that should begin with a consonant cluster.

CURRICULUM LINKS
NLS: Y1, T2, Word level 3.

What's missing?

What you need
A whiteboard or flipchart; marker pens.

What to do
● Write the word *back* on the flipchart or whiteboard and invite the children to read it to you. Say, *Oh dear, my spelling isn't very good today. I've missed out a letter near the beginning of the word. I meant to write a word that is a colour. Can you guess what I wanted to write?*

● Write the word *black* on the chart, underlining the second consonant. Tell the children that you missed out the letter *l*. Can anyone suggest which sound in the word *black* you forgot to write a sound for?

● Now explain that you will write some more words on the flipchart, telling the children what you intended to spell. Ask the children to check that you have written what you think you have, or if you have left out any more letters.

● Write the following words on the chart, giving the related clues to indicate what the words should be. Say each time, *I wanted to write a word that means…* For example, write *cab* and say: *I wanted to write a word that means a sea creature with claws.*

    tap: something you use to catch someone or something
    fog: an animal that croaks and lives in a pond
    sip: to slide on ice and fall down
    cap: hit your hands together to show you have enjoyed something
    fat: smooth, not bumpy
    sick: small piece of wood
    suck: fixed with glue
    tack: a train runs along this

● Each time the children give the correct word, invite them to tell you which sound you have forgotten to write and which letter you should have used to write it.

Differentiation
With younger children, sound out the word you intended to write, asking one child to point to the letters in the word you have written. This will help to make it clear which sound is missing and where it should be in the word. As you give the clues to your intended words, invite older and more able children to write the correct words down rather than just say them and check their answers at the end of the list.

AGE RANGE 6–7

LEARNING OBJECTIVE
To build a range of words using given initial consonant clusters and a series of word endings.

CURRICULUM LINKS
NLS: Y1, T2, Word level 3.

Which blend?

What you need
Paper; pencils; 20 pieces of thin card measuring 5cm by 3cm; 16 pieces of differently coloured card measuring 2cm by 3cm; four envelopes.

What to do
● Write one of the word endings below on each of the larger pieces of card, keeping the pattern to the right-hand side of the card to allow a smaller piece to be superimposed to form the beginning of a word.

–ick	–amp	–ash	–im
–ack	–and	–ink	–ot
–ock	–op	–ock	–ap
–ash	–ump	–ot	–unk
–at	–ick	–ap	–amp

● Divide the cards into four sets and store each in one of the envelopes.
● Make four sets of initial consonant clusters, by writing the blends *tr*, *cl*, *st* and *fl* on the smaller pieces of card, four times over. Add a set of blends to each envelope.
● Invite four children to play a game. Give each child an envelope, a piece of paper and a pencil. Ask the children to lay out their word ending cards in a column on the table in front of them. Explain that they are going to try to build words by placing one of the consonant clusters in front of each of their endings in turn. They should write down any real words that they make on their piece of paper.
● Encourage the children to choose a cluster and try it with the first of their word endings.
● Explain that when they have tried the first blend with all of the endings, they should try to build words using another cluster. Challenge them to find out which of the consonant clusters will make real words with every one of their endings. When they have found this out, they should write the cluster at the top of their list of words.

Differentiation
With younger children, work on one set of endings as a group, reading out each word ending and encouraging the children to blend the initial cluster with these. Scribe the words for the children. Encourage older and more able children to swap envelopes, so that they all work through each of the sets of endings. Then ask them to compare their conclusions about which blend could make words with all the endings in each set.

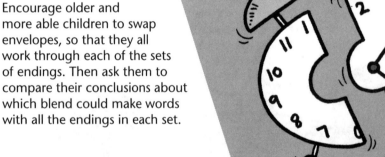

Phonic Fun!

AGE RANGE 6–7

LEARNING OBJECTIVE
To decide whether a particular final consonant cluster can be used with a range of word beginnings to make real words.

CURRICULUM LINKS
NLS: Y1, T2, Word level 3.

Blend the end

What you need
Three 4cm squares of thin card for each child; 30 A5 pieces of card; pencils; flipchart; marker pen.

What to do
● Write one of the word beginnings listed below on each piece of A5 card in large lower case letters. Keep the two letters to the left of the card with an underlined space for writing on the right.

(Set 1)	(Set 2)	(Set 3)
–nd / –nt	**–st / –sk**	**–lt / –ld**
be__	ne__	me__
la__	ri__	ho__
wi__	re__	be__
hu__	tu__	hi__
sa__	be__	bo__
le__	ve__	fo__
te__	de__	he__
hi__	hu__	so__
sta__	ma__	pe__
mi__	fl__	chi__

● Give each child three pieces of card. Invite them to write a cross on one piece and a tick on each of the others.
● Explain to the children that they are going to help you build words by deciding which of two endings can be used with some word beginnings to make real words.
● Divide the flipchart into two columns. Write –nd at the top of one column and –nt at the top of the second. Invite the children to sound out these endings.
● Hold up the first card from Set 1. Say, *This is the beginning of a word. It says 'be__'. I want you to decide if I can add this '–nd' pattern* (point to the '–nd') *to make a real word. If I can, put a tick card on the table. If I can't, put a cross card down.*
● Read the card again, this time pointing to the –nt pattern. Say, *Can I add the '–nt' pattern to this to make a word? Choose a tick or a cross card to put next to the first card.*
● Write the words *bend* and *bent* in the appropriate columns, then ask the children to check if they had two tick cards on the table. Explain that sometimes only one word will be made.
● Work through the set before moving on to Set 2 and Set 3.

Differentiation
For younger children, write the final clusters on smaller pieces of card and place them onto the right-hand side of the A5 cards. Help the children to blend the beginning and ending together before they decide whether it is a real word.
Invite older and more able children
to read the word beginnings
themselves, letting them
write the words rather than
using the tick and cross
cards.

AGE RANGE 6–7

LEARNING OBJECTIVE
To use clues to add or remove letters from words to spell a series of words with a long *ie* sound.

CURRICULUM LINKS
NLS: Y2, T3, Word level 1.

Add/take away/ switch

What you need
Pencils; paper.

What to do
● Explain to the children that you would like them to solve a series of riddles. Tell them that you are going to give them a clue to a word. The word will have the sound *ie* in it, and they must write that word down. You will then give them an instruction.

● Write the words *Add*, *Take away* and *Switch* on the board.

● Tell the children that if you say *Add*, they will need to add one or more letters to the first word to find the second.

● If you say *Take away*, they will need to remove one or more letters.

● If you say *Switch*, they should change the order of the letters to get the next word.

● Explain that two instructions may be combined, so they will need to listen very carefully.

● Tell the children that, as well as the instruction, you will give them a clue to the second word, which will have the same *ie* sound in it. This will continue until they have written five words.

● Work through the first sequence of clues, checking the children's answers to the first two clues to make sure that they have understood what is required.

> You wear it round your neck   _ _ _   (*tie*)
> **Add**
> Held together with string   _ _ _ _   (*tied*)
> **Add and Switch**
> The sea comes in and goes out   _ _ _ _ _   (*tides*)
> **Take away and Switch**
> Not the front or the back but the   _ _ _ _   (*side*)
> **Switch**
> Stops living   _ _ _ _   (*dies*)

● Check the children's answers at the end of the sequence and then try the following set of words:

> To tell an untruth   _ _ _   (*lie*)
> **Add and Switch**
> A measurement of distance   _ _ _ _   (*mile*)
> **Switch**
> Like a lemon but green   _ _ _ _   (*lime*)
> **Add and Switch**
> To look happy   _ _ _ _ _   (*smile*)
> **Switch**
> An oozing wet mess   _ _ _ _ _   (*slime*)

Differentiation
List the answers and invite younger children to find the correct word to match the clue, or cue the children with the correct number of dashes on the board (as indicated above) to help them work out the word. Challenge older and more able children to work out the clues and correct instructions for the sequence: *pie, ripe, tripe, stripe, strip*.

AGE RANGE 7–8

LEARNING OBJECTIVE
To solve clues in order to spell sets of words with a common *ie* sound, one word of which is spelled with a different pattern.

CURRICULUM LINKS
NLS: Y3, T1, T2, T3, Word level 1.

Odd man out

What you need
A whiteboard; marker pen; pencils; paper.

What to do
● Tell the children that you are going to give them clues to groups of three words that begin with the same letter. Explain that they must work out the words to answer the clues and then decide which of the three is the odd word out.
● Give the first set of clues, asking the children to write down the three answer words:
 You turn it on when it gets dark (*light*)
 You use a ruler to draw a … (*line*)
 If you enjoy something you … doing it (*like*)
● Apart from the first sound in those words, ask the children if there is another sound which they all have in common? Then invite them to tell you whether the *ie* sound is spelled the same in all three words. So, can they tell you which is the odd man out?
● Write their answer on the board.
● Now try a second set of words:
 Ten take away one makes … (*nine*)
 A word which means pleasant (*nice*)
 Opposite of day (*night*)
● Again, invite the children to compare the sounds and spellings in the words, writing the odd man out on the board.
● Make up clues for further sets of words:

fight	mine	tide	side
file	mice	tight	sight
fine	might	tile	site

● Invite the children to look at the list of 'odd men out'. Do they notice a common pattern after the *igh* spelling of the long *ie* sound?
● Point out that the sound *ite* at the end of short words will be spelled with an *ight* pattern more often that with an *ite* pattern.

Differentiation
Prompt younger children by giving the initial letter for each set of answers and explain to them before giving the clues that all the words have a long *ie* sound in them, spelled either with *i–e* or with *igh*. Challenge older children to discover two *igh* pattern words in which this pattern is not followed by the letter *t* (*high* / *sigh*), and to explore which short words do use the *ite* pattern.

AGE RANGE 7–8

LEARNING OBJECTIVE
To correctly pair two halves of a sentence, using words with matching spelling patterns for the vowel *er* sound as a cue.

CURRICULUM LINKS
NLS: Y3, T1, T2, T3, Word level 2.

Pair it

What you need
Whiteboard or flipchart; marker pen; paper; pencils.

What to do
● Transcribe the following sentence halves onto a whiteboard or flipchart:

The girl wore a matching blue skirt	served at seven o'clock.
The clowns in the circus	he had to swerve suddenly.
If you are hurt	lurking behind the bushes.
The driver was shocked when	stop it burning.
The police found the burglar	of hairy spiders.
The bird sat on a branch	and a blue shirt.
Turn the toast to	and twirl.
My sister is very scared	chirping loudly.
The dancer started to whirl	you may need a nurse.
I think that dinner will be	squirted water at each other.

● Explain to the children that the sentence halves have become jumbled and that you would like them to pair the correct halves with one another.
● Tell them that every sentence half contains a word with an *er* sound in it. Point to three sentence halves in which the *er* sound is spelled in different ways, inviting the children to pick out some of these words for you.
● Ask, *Can you find me a word with an 'er' sound here?* Underline the words. Say, *Is that sound spelled in the same way in all of those words?*
● Now invite the children to begin matching the sentence halves and to write down their full sentences on paper. Explain that each half of a sentence must contain a word with the *er* sound spelled in the same way as the matching half, and that the whole sentence must make sense.

Differentiation
Work with individual younger children. Make a photocopy of the sentence halves for each child. Help them to underline the words with *er* sounds, colour-coding the three different spellings. Let them draw lines to link sentence halves. Then scribe the completed sentences onto the flipchart for them.

Ask older and more able children to make three lists of the words containing the *er* sound according to the spelling pattern, and to add as many other words as they can to each list.

Phonic Fun!   BRIGHT IDEAS

AGE RANGE 7–8

LEARNING OBJECTIVE
To spell a range of words using different patterns for the long *ai* sound.

CURRICULUM LINKS
NLS: Y3, T1, T2, T3, Word level 1.

Frame it

What you need
The 'Frame it' photocopiable sheet on page 71; pencils.

What to do
● Make one copy of the photocopiable sheet for each child.

● Explain to the children that they are going to complete some puzzles. Invite them to look at the sheets, and tell them that they must use the clues on the right to help them complete the grid on the left of the page.

● Tell the children that all of the answers to the clues on the page will be words which have the same sound in them. Suggest that you try the first few clues to see if they can work out what the common sound in the words might be.

● Work together on the first three clues before asking the children to tell you which sound they can hear in all of the words. Is the sound spelled with the same pattern in those three words?

● Explain to the children that this long *ai* sound can be written with eight different patterns. As part of this activity they will be finding out how many of those patterns occur in the word puzzles. They will also be discovering which other word containing the long *ai* sound they have framed in the special boxes.

● Invite the children to continue filling in the puzzles. The answers (with the framed letters highlighted in bold) are:

w **e** i g h	**r** e i n
r a **i** n	b r e **a** k
a **g** e	p l a **i** n
h a i l	f l **a** m e
g a **t** e	**w** a g e
o b **e** y	s p **a** d e
v **e** i n	g r e **y**
p a **n** e	

Differentiation
Work thorough all the clues with younger children, cueing them with the correct spelling pattern for any given word if they are experiencing difficulty. Challenge older children to think of any other words which spell the long *ai* sound with the patterns *ey* and *ea* (*prey*, *they*, *great*, *steak*), explaining that this is a rare pattern.

AGE RANGE 7–8

LEARNING OBJECTIVE
To identify the correct spelling pattern for the *oa* sound in a range of words.

CURRICULUM LINKS
NLS: Y3, T1, T2, T3, Word level 1.

Does your toe know?

What you need
A sheet of A3 paper for each child; pencils; coloured pencils; marker pens.

What to do
● Make a copy of the following poem and photocopy it for each child.

A silly old goat, afloat on a moat,
just didn't see a hole in his boat.
'I really don't know
why this boat is so slow.
I have tried hard to row,
but it simply won't go.'
Then over Goat's toes,
right up to his nose,
the cold water rose,
and seeped through his clothes.
It soaked through the coat
of the silly old goat,
and he started to croak,
'This isn't a joke!'

© *Jillian Harker*

● Explain to the children that the poem includes a number of words that contain the same sound. Invite them to find four such words in the first line. Ask them to say the sound and whether it is spelled the same in all four words.
● Invite the children to read the poem, underlining any words with an *oa* sound in pencil. Next, ask them to underline or highlight the words in one of four different colours, according to the pattern used to spell the *oa* sound.
● Give each child a sheet of A3 paper. Ask them to tell you what the four spelling patterns they found were, and to write one pattern in the middle of each side of the paper in marker pen. Ensure that they write all of the patterns the same way up.
● Invite the children to stand in the middle of their paper in a space. Explain that you are going to read the poem to them, and that each time they hear a word with an *o* sound they must move onto the pattern that would be used to spell it in the word they heard.
● Read the poem at a slightly slowed rate.

Differentiation
For younger children, use one master copy of the poem and work through it as a group, underlining and highlighting the words. When reading the poem, provide a model of the movements onto the correct patterns for the children to copy. With older children, do not indicate how many different patterns there are, but encourage the children to work it out. Read the poem at normal speed.

See also: Sound snap (p81).

Phonic Fun! **BRIGHT IDEAS**

AGE RANGE 7–8

LEARNING OBJECTIVE
To use clues to spell sets of words containing the long oo sound, each set having a common spelling pattern.

CURRICULUM LINKS
NLS:Y3, T1, T2, T3, Word level 1.

New clues

What you need
Paper; pencils.

What to do
● Explain to the children that you are going to give them clues to some words. All the words that are answers to the clues will have the sound *oo* in them. Tell them that you will give the clues in sets of five, and all five words will have that sound spelled in the same way. The next set of words will have the same sound, but spelled in a different way. Explain that they must write their answers down and, at the end of each set of words, you will ask them what their answers are and how they have spelled the *oo* sound in that set of words.

● Work through the first set of clues:
Shines in the sky at night (*moon*)
Knife, fork and ...? (*spoon*)
You swim in it (*pool*)
On top of a house (*roof*)
Noise that an owl makes (*hoot*).

● Ask the children how they have spelt the *oo* sound in those words.

● Now work though the other sets of clues, checking at the end of each list which pattern the words have in common.

Not polite (*rude*)	A day of the week (*Tuesday*)
Very, very big (*huge*)	A colour (*blue*)
A month of the year (*June*)	Sticky stuff (*glue*)
A musical instrument (*flute*)	Not a lie (*true*)
Played on an instrument (*tune*)	A hint (*clue*)

Not old (*new*)	Apples, bananas, pears (*fruit*)
Precious stone (*jewel*)	Holiday on a boat (*cruise*)
Team of workers on a boat (*crew*)	Black and blue mark on skin (*bruise*)
A way of eating (*chew*)	Matching jacket and trousers (*suit*)
Turn it to fix a piece of wood (*screw*)	Squeeze it from an orange (*juice*)

● Invite the children to explore with you which patterns occur at the end of words or syllables, and which occur in the middle of syllables.

Differentiation
Cue younger children with the correct spelling pattern for the words in each set, before giving the clues. Invite older and more able children to try to add other words to the sets, and to comment upon which patterns appear to be more common than others.

How does it sound?

AGE RANGE 7–8

LEARNING OBJECTIVE
To find words with the pattern *ou* or *ow* in a wordsearch.

CURRICULUM LINKS
NLS: Y3, T1, T2, T3, Word level 6.

What you need
The 'How does it sound?' photocopiable sheet on page 72; pens or hightlighter pens.

What to do
● Make one copy of the photocopiable sheet for each child.

● Explain to the children that they are going to try to find words in the wordsearch which have either an *ow* or an *ou* pattern. Encourage the children to look for examples of the patterns and to build words around these. Try two or three examples together before asking the children to hunt out the remaining words.

● Now encourage the children to look at the clues beneath the wordsearch and to try to fit each of the words that they have discovered to a clue. When they have done this, check the answers:

sleepy (*drowsy*)	a noise (*sound*)
not up (*down*)	100 pence (*pound*)
dress (*gown*)	a circle (*round*)
sink in water (*drown*)	earth (*ground*)
bigger than village (*town*)	not in (*out*)
king's hat (*crown*)	noisy (*loud*)
bird of prey (*owl*)	seen in sky (*cloud*)
noise of dog (*growl*)	to jump on (*pounce*)
to stalk (*prowl*)	1,2,3,4,5 (*count*)

● Discuss with the children whether the two patterns in these words make the same sound. If you have previously used the activity 'Bobo the clown' on page 48, encourage the children to check whether the words from the wordsearch fit the pattern they discovered in that activity for choosing between the two patterns for the *ow* sound when spelling.

Differentiation
Work with younger children to discover all of the words, encouraging them to look through the wordsearch in a logical order, scanning each row first and then each column. Provide a set of further *ou* and *ow* words for older and more able children, inviting them to create their own wordsearch and clues.

Phonic Fun! **BRIGHT IDEAS**

AGE RANGE 8–9

LEARNING OBJECTIVE
To distinguish pairs of homophones with an *air* sound in a nonsense string and to place these words correctly in a cloze exercise.

CURRICULUM LINKS
NLS: Y4, T1, Word level 6.

Hide and seek

What you need
Pencils.

What to do
● Make a master of the following puzzles and cloze exercise. Photocopy the master for each child:

```
f a f a i r f o t f a b f a r e f o d
h a n i m a h a i r h a r e d e n
w e a r c w o m i v u w a r e
t e l s t a r e k i s t a i r l e t o f i
a l i t f l a r e o l f l a i r m f e l
d e b a r e d i b o b e a r d u n
g u n i p o p e a r u p a i r y i p
```

She did not have enough money to pay her _ _ _ _ on the bus.

She had long _ _ _ _ hair.

I washed my _ _ _ _ last night.

A _ _ _ _ looks a bit like a rabbit.

My friend likes to _ _ _ _ bright clothes.

Dad bought a hammer in the hard _ _ _ _ shop.

She fell from the top _ _ _ _ to the bottom.

It is very rude to _ _ _ _ at people.

My brother has a _ _ _ _ for making things.

They lit a _ _ _ _ to help the rescuers find them.

I still keep my teddy _ _ _ _ by my bed.

_ _ _ _ skin can burn easily in hot sun.

Today I have an apple and a _ _ _ _ in my lunch box.

Do you like my new _ _ _ _ of shoes?

● Explain to the children that there are two real words hidden in each of the nonsense strings and that both words in a string will be homophones. Check that the children understand that homophones are words which sound the same but have different meanings and different spellings.
● Invite the children to find the pair of homophones in the first string. When they have found the words, encourage them to find the appropriate sentence in which to fit each word to show its correct meaning.
● Invite them to work through the remaining puzzles in this way.

Differentiation
Tell younger children which words they are looking for, and ask them to underline them in the nonsense string. Discuss the meaning of each of the homophones before asking the children to place these in the appropriate sentence. For older and more able children, provide other pairs of homophones and invite the children to conceal these in nonsense strings and create sentences for each other to work on.

AGE RANGE 7–9

LEARNING OBJECTIVE
To use the spelling of a known word to spell other words for which clues have been given.

CURRICULUM LINKS
NLS: Y3, T1, T2, T3, Word level 6; Y4, T1, T2, T3, Word level 3.

Chains

What you need
Paper; pencils.

What to do
● Explain to the children that you are going to give them a set of clues so that they can create a chain of words which all contain the same spelling pattern.

● Tell them that all of the words will have two syllables, and that the second syllable will end with the sound *ee*, which will be spelled the same way in each word.

● Invite the children to write the first word in the chain. Say, *Start with something that bees make.* Check that they have all written the word *honey*, discussing how they have spelt the final *ee* sound. Tell the children that there is a reasonably small group of words which uses this spelling pattern, then give the following clues to the children:

1) Change the first letter for something you spend (*money*)
2) Add another letter for a type of ape (*monkey*)
3) Change the first letter for an animal you can ride on (*donkey*)
4) Change the first and third letter for a game played with sticks and a ball (*hockey*)
5) Change the first letter for someone who rides a horse (*jockey*)
6) Remove three letters for something that locks a door (*key*)
7) Add three letters for a bird eaten at Christmas (*turkey*).

● Now invite the children to use what they know about this spelling pattern to solve some other clues and spell more words:

1) A warm jumper (*jersey*)
2) A big dip between two hills (*valley*)
3) A trip to somewhere (*journey*)
4) Monks live in one of these (*abbey*)
5) To hit a ball before it bounces (*volley*)
6) Smoke comes from this on the roof of a house (*chimney*)
7) This has a rope round it which helps to move something (*pulley*)
8) An organ of the body that cleans the blood (*kidney*).

Differentiation
Give younger children the *ey* spelling pattern at the outset and work through the first set of clues only, building the chain together. Challenge older and more able children to discover other spelling patterns for the *ee* sound which can be found at the ends of words.

AGE RANGE 8–9

LEARNING OBJECTIVE
To identify different spelling patterns for the various long vowel sounds.

CURRICULUM LINKS
NLS: Y4, T1, T2, T3, Word level 3.

Sounds the same

What you need
Flipchart; marker pen; paper; pencils.

What to do
● Write the following list of words on the flipchart:
gate, tie, true, key, wait, height, try, moan, cone, ceiling, grey, you, sigh, bee, slow, flea, eight, knew, open, unit.
● Explain to the children that each of these words contains one of the long vowel sounds. Tell them that their task will be to sort out these 20 words into five groups of four words, according to the vowel sounds in the word.
● Tell the children that they will need to decide whether the vowel sound (or the first vowel sound if there is more than one) is:

an 'ai' sound, like in 'train'
an 'ee' sound, like in 'meet'
an 'ie' sound, like in 'light'
an 'oa' sound, like in 'boat'
or an 'oo' sound, like in 'blue'

● Ask the children to divide their paper into three columns, and to write '*ai' sound* at the top of the first column, *spelled* at the top of the second column and *also found in* at the top of the third column.
● Invite the children to tell you the first word that they can see which contains an *ai* sound, and to write it in the first column. Explain that in the second column, you would like them to write the pattern that spells the *ai* sound in that word. For the third column, they will need to think of another word that uses that same pattern to spell an *ai* sound.
● Now invite the children to find the other three words with an *ai* sound, explaining that the sound will be spelled differently in each of the four words. Ask them to add the spelling pattern in the second column each time, and another word that uses the pattern in the third column.
For example:

'ai 'sound	spelled	also found in
gate	a–e	name
wait	ai	rain
eight	eigh	weight
grey	ey	they

● Work through each of the long vowel sounds in this way.

Differentiation
With younger children, omit the final column and help them to extract the correct spelling pattern from each word once they have sorted out the words with the same vowel sound. Challenge older and more able children to think of three more words that use each pattern, rather then one.

AGE RANGE 8–9

LEARNING OBJECTIVE
To sort a range of words into categories and to list them according to the number of syllables they contain.

CURRICULUM LINKS
NLS: Y4, T1, T2, T3, Word level 1.

One, two, three, four, five

What you need
A flipchart; marker pen, paper; pencils.

What to do
● Explain to the children that they are going to carry out an exercise to count the syllables in words.
● Write the word *banana* on the chart, asking the children to count the vowels in the word. Invite them to say the word, comparing the number of vowels and syllables.
● Now carry out the same procedure with the word *beetroot*. Explain that although there are four vowels in this word, they come together in two pairs. Every syllable in English must have at least one vowel or a vowel pair, so counting the vowels or vowel pairs in a word can help us to work out the number of syllables.
● Next, write the word *Greece* on the chart, saying the word as you do so. Invite the children to tell you how many syllables they hear. Point out that a silent *e* at the end of a word is not heard and is not included when counting syllables.
● Finally, write the word *lion* on the chart. Explain that this has two syllables because two vowels which are next to eachother sometimes make separate sounds, rather than working together. Say that the combinations *io* and *ia* are examples of this.
● Now write all the words listed below on the chart in a random order:

vegetables	flowers	animals	countries
sprout	rose	cow	France
cabbage	tulip	donkey	England
aubergine	daffodil	crocodile	America
cauliflower	dandelion	rhinoceros	Indonesia
		hippopotamus	Czechoslovakia

● Invite the children to sort them out into categories first of all, under the headings given in bold.
● When they have sorted the words into groups, ask the children to use what they know about syllables to help them put the words in each group in order, starting with the word with one syllable, then two syllables, and so on.

Differentiation
Scribe for younger children as you sort out the words. Read each word out and encourage the children to place their hands (palms down) lightly under their chins as they repeat each word. Counting how many times their chin pushes against their hands will help them decide the number of syllables. Challenge older and more able children to create other lists using different categories of words, such as sports or means of transport.

See also: Syllable scramble (p88).

Phonic Fun! **BRIGHT IDEAS**

Three in one

Task 1
Read these words.

can	rub	cup	mad	let	fan
big	hop	sit	jam	kit	lit
hum	bun	bob	pat	quit	rat
sun	fat	run	van	wet	box
yet	zip				

Task 2
Find three words with each of the following rhyming patterns:

–un	–et	–at	–an	–it
___	___	___	___	___
___	___	___	___	___
___	___	___	___	___

Task 3
Now go back to the list of words at the top of the page.
Underline one letter in each word, beginning with 'a',
then 'b', 'c', 'd' and so on, until you have found
the whole alphabet.

Missing middle

```
      a
c <      > t
      o
```
_____

```
      u
c <      > p
      a
```
_____

```
      o
l <      > g
      e
```
_____

```
      e
p <      > g
      i
```
_____

```
      i
t <      > p
      a
```
_____

```
      a
c <      > t
      u
```
_____

```
      a
m <      > n
      e
```
_____

```
      e
p <      > n
      i
```
_____

```
      a
l <      > p
      i
```
_____

Phonic Fun!   **BRIGHT IDEAS**

Frame it

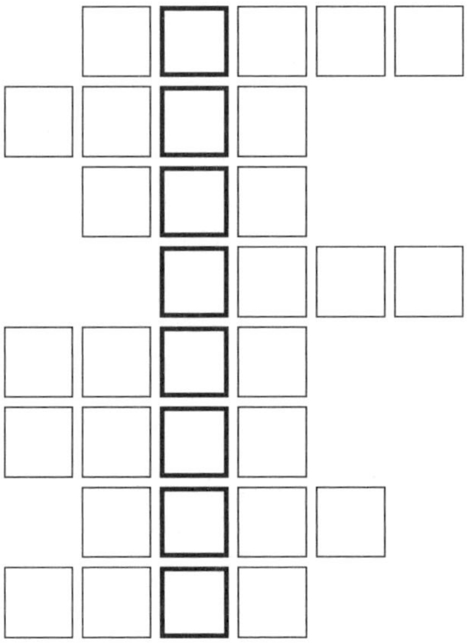

Check how heavy something is

Wet drops falling from the sky

How old you are

Frozen drops falling from the sky

Go through this into the garden

Carry out orders

Blood flows through this

Glass in a window

Which word have you framed?

_____

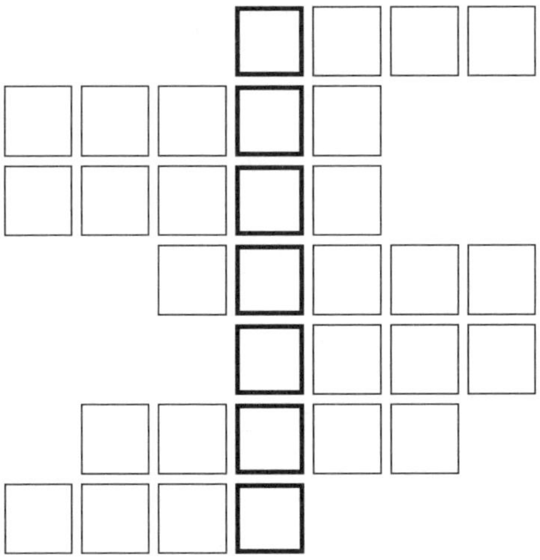

Use it to control a horse

Smash

Not patterned

Found in a fire

Paid for a job

Use it to dig with

Drab colour

Which word have you framed?

_____

● How many different ways can you see to spell the long 'ai' sound?

How does it sound?

● Search for the words with an 'ou' or 'ow' pattern. Write your answers next to the correct clues.

l	o	u	d	s	y	r	n
s	u	w	r	o	u	n	d
c	t	p	o	u	n	c	e
o	g	o	w	n	b	q	u
u	r	u	s	d	o	w	n
n	o	n	y	c	t	o	c
t	u	d	g	r	o	w	l
f	n	p	r	o	w	l	o
l	d	r	o	w	n	a	u
c	e	a	j	n	g	y	d

sleepy _____   a noise _____

not up _____   100 pence _____

dress _____   a circle _____

sink in water _____   earth _____

bigger than village _____   not in _____

bird of prey _____   noisy _____

king's hat? _____   seen in sky _____

noise of dog _____   to jump on _____

to stalk _____   1,2,3,4,5 _____

● Do the 'ou' and 'ow' patterns make the same sound or different sounds in these words?

CHAPTER 4

Games and puzzles

AGE RANGE 5–7

LEARNING OBJECTIVE
To reinforce awareness that words which end with rhyming sounds are likely to have matching letter patterns.

CURRICULUM LINKS
NLS: YR, Word level 4.

Families

What you need
44 pieces of thin card measuring 5cm by 7cm; marker pen.

What to do
● Make sets of rhyming cards by writing one CVC word from the following groups on each piece of card:

man	hog	cat	net	red	peg	bag	kit	lip	bug	bun
can	fog	rat	pet	bed	leg	rag	lit	dip	mug	run
fan	dog	hat	wet	fed	keg	tag	sit	hip	tug	fun
pan	log	mat	set	ted	beg	wag	bit	pip	hug	sun

● Choose enough cards for each child in your group to have one. Make the sets smaller if necessary to create evenly-sized 'family' groups.
● Shuffle the cards and deal them out to the children. Encourage the children to look at their word and to work out what it says. Explain that you are going to choose someone to read the word on their card out loud. Say that everyone else should listen carefully to see if the word that is read out rhymes with the word on their card.
● Invite one child to read out their card and then say, *We need <u>three</u> more cards for a family. Put up your hand if you rhyme with me.* (Adjust the number if you are using smaller rhyming sets.)
● Encourage the children who think they have a rhyming card to put up their hand. Invite each child to read out their word, responding, as appropriate, *Yes that word rhymes, I do agree. Come and sit with your family* or *That doesn't rhyme. I don't agree. You can't sit with this family.*
● When a child reads out a word that does rhyme, invite them to come and sit with their family group.
● When all of the children have found their families, shuffle the cards or choose new sets, and begin the game again.

Differentiation
Work with smaller groups of younger children, using pairs of cards only, and help the children to sound out their words before the game begins. Encourage older children to make sets of words with initial or final consonant clusters.

AGE RANGE 5–7

LEARNING OBJECTIVE
To provide practice in manipulation of phonemes in CVC words.

CURRICULUM LINKS
NLS: Y1, T1, Word level 1 and 4.

All change

What you need
26 pieces of thin card measuring 5cm by 7cm (six of one colour and 20 of another); pen.

What to do
● Prepare two sets of cards. Use the six pieces of card for the first set, and write one of the following instructions on each card:
   Change the first sound to make a new word.
   Change the last sound to make a new word.
   Change the middle sound to make a new word.
   Think of a word with the same first sound.
   Think of a word with the same last sound.
   Think of a word with the same middle sound.
● Next, write one of the following words on each of the cards in the second set:

cup	jet	sit	box
net	top	man	hat
pen	fun	hog	cap
log	pip	jug	bed
hen	bug	fan	bus

● Place both sets of cards face down on the table then invite a group of up to five children to play a game.
● Explain to the children that they are going to take turns to pick up one card from the 'word' pile and one card from the 'instruction' pile. Invite one child to start the game by picking a card from each pile.
● Encourage the child to read out the word out and to show you the instruction card.

● Read the instruction to the child, adding, *Can you do that with the word you have just read out to me?*
● Place the instruction card at the bottom of the pile. If the child was able to make a new word, then they can keep the word card. If not, they should place it at the bottom of the word card pile.
● Move around the group letting each child take a turn until all the word cards have been won. The winner of the game is the child with the most word cards.

Differentiation
For younger children, remove the instructions about medial sounds and offer two alternative answers from which to choose, if they are finding it difficult to construct answers independently. Suggest older and more able children to think of more CVC words to add to the word pile. Encourage them to play with the words first to discover whether they can make new words, using any of the instructions.

Phonic Fun!

AGE RANGE 5–7

LEARNING OBJECTIVE
To practice segmenting the phonemes in CVC words in order to construct and write new, linked words.

CURRICULUM LINKS
NLS: Y1, T1, Word level 6.

Round and round the garden

What you need
The 'Round and Round the Garden' photocopiable sheet on page 89; thin card; counters; pencils; paper.

What to do
● Make one copy of the photocopiable sheet onto thin card for each child.
● Give each child their copy of the game board, a piece of paper, a pencil and a counter. Explain that they are going to play a word game.
● Invite the children to decide on a stepping stone from which to begin the game. This can be any stone around the board. Ask them to place a counter on their chosen stepping stone and to write down the word for that picture on their piece of paper. Help the children if they are not clear what the word should be. Starting at the top left hand corner and moving anticlockwise, the words are as follows: hat, cat, can, cap, tap, tag, bag, beg, leg, log, hog, hop and hot.
● Now invite the children to move their counter onto the next stepping stone and write down the word for the new picture, underneath the first word. Explain that they only need to change one letter in the first word to make the second word.
● Encourage the children to move round the board in this way until they reach the stone on which they first started. Ensure that they understand that they need to change only one letter each time they move to make the new word.

Differentiation
Work in a smaller group with younger children, using one enlarged photocopy of the game board and alphabet bricks or cubes, arranged on the table in an arc. Build the first word with the alphabet letters, then invite the children to take turns to change the appropriate letter to make the new word before they write it down, using the alphabet letters as a model. Invite more able children to experiment with starting on a new stepping stone or going round the board in the opposite direction, to see if they need to change one letter only in every case when they move on. Encourage them to try to build their own short word circles.

AGE RANGE 5–7

LEARNING OBJECTIVE
To blend three phonemes together to read simple words and to experiment with medial letters to decide which will make a real word.

CURRICULUM LINKS
NLS: Y1, T1, Word level 5.

Five in a hive

What you need
The 'Five in a hive' photocopiable sheet on page 90; thin card; two sets of bee counters (see photocopiable); two dice.

What to do
● Copy the photocopiable sheet on to thin card to make a game board. Make two sets of five bee counters. Colour one set yellow and the other orange.
● Invite two children to play a game. Give each child a set of counters. Explain that the aim of the game is to get all of their bees back to the hive. Point out the five vowels written on the counters, telling the children that the counters can only land on a 'flower' where the vowel will make a real word.
● Encourage the first child to roll the two dice. Tell the child that they can either add the scores together to move one bee counter, or use each score to move a different counter. Explain that the children can have up to five counters on the board at any one time. Encourage the first child to count along to the appropriate flower(s) and ask, *Which vowels could you use to make real words here?* Invite them to choose the appropriate counters to place on the flowers.
● Now let the second child throw the dice. Point out that counters cannot be placed on flowers that already have a counter on them, and help the child to decide the best way to use the throw with this in mind. Encourage the children to read the words that they are building with each turn.
● Help the children to explore whether it is possible to move two counters in any one go, or if they need to combine the scores to move only one. As they near the hive, explain that they must throw exactly the right number to move each vowel bee from the flowers onto its final position around the hive.
● The winner is the first player to move all of their five bees into position around the hive.

Differentiation
For younger and less able children, use only one or two vowel counters at a time to move around the board and help the children to sound out the three phonemes first each time, before blending them into a word. Ask more able children to write down a list of all the words that they have made as they moved around the board and to read them back to you.

Phonic Fun!

AGE RANGE 5–7

LEARNING OBJECTIVE
To practise reading a range of words with the long
oo (moon) and the short *oo* (book) sounds.

CURRICULUM LINKS
NLS: Y2, T3, Word level 6.

Line up

What you need
The 'Line up' photocopiable sheet on page 91; two sets of counters in different colours; whiteboard; dry-wipe marker pen.

What to do
● Write the words *moon* and *book* on a whiteboard. Write the pattern *oo* beneath the words. Ask the children, *Does this pattern make the same sound in the words 'moon' and 'book'?*
● Now write *food* and *cool* on the board, inviting the children to tell you whether the *oo* pattern makes the same sound as it did in *moon* or as in *book*. Do the same with *look* and *wood*.
● Show the children the game board and explain that they will be reading lots of *oo* words as they play this game. Remind them that this pattern can make two different sounds.
● Invite the children to choose a set of counters. Explain that the first player can choose to read any word on the board. If they read it correctly, they can cover the word with one of their counters. The second player then chooses a word to read and cover.
● Tell the children that the aim of the game is to cover four words in a row. Explain that the rows can be vertical, horizontal or diagonal, and use counters on the board to illustrate what you mean.
● Invite the first player to read a word and to place their counter on the board. When the second player has taken a turn, make sure that the children understand that they need to keep a check on their opponent's counters as well as their own. Explain that they may need to read a particular word to block their opponent's line, rather than choosing a word that they want to read.
● Several pairs of players can play the game at the same time, using one game board per pair, and checking with an adult if they are not sure that they have read a certain word correctly. The winner is the first player to make a line of four counters.

Differentiation
For younger children, use a red pen to underline the *oo* pattern on the game board for words with the long (moon) sound, and a blue pen to underline the *oo* pattern for words with the short (book) sound. Explain how this will help them to know which sound the *oo* makes in the words. Invite older children to list the words from the game in two groups, according to the sound of the *oo* pattern.

AGE RANGE 6–7

LEARNING OBJECTIVE
To practise blending consonant clusters and common word endings to read a range of words.

CURRICULUM LINKS
NLS: Y1, T2, Word level 3.

Blend it

What you need
The 'Blend it' photocopiable sheet on page 92; thin card; 30 blank pieces of card; dice; counters.

What to do
● Copy the photocopiable sheet onto thin card to make a game board.
● Write one of the following word endings on each of the 30 blank pieces of card:

ap	ass	ink	ake	out
ip	ess	ack	ide	ain
op	ash	ick	eak	ow
at	ush	uck	eam	own
ot	ing	eep	eat	ight
in	ank	eet	ay	ew

● Invite up to four children to play the game. Shuffle the word cards and deal three cards to each player. Ask the children to spread their cards on the table in front of them and check that they can all read each of the endings on their cards.
● Ask the children to roll the dice in turn. Whoever rolls the highest score should go first. Explain that the children are going to take turns to roll the dice and move their counter along the squares, in the direction of the arrows.
● Explain that when they land on a square, they must try to build a word using the consonant cluster on that square and one of their word endings. If they can use one of their cards to build a word they must tell everyone what that word is. They should then place the card that they have used face down on the bottom of the pile and pick up another card from the top. Tell the children that they must say the word that they are building before placing the card back in the pile.
● Invite each child to throw the dice in turn. If one of the children is unable to build a word using any of their three cards, then they must choose one card to put back at the bottom of the pack, take another from the top and pass the dice to the next player without taking another turn.
● If any of the players lands on a starred square, then they can have another turn. The winner is the player who reaches the finish first.

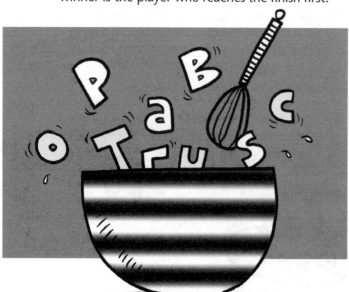

Differentiation
Simplify for younger children by leaving out the final set of endings from the list above. Encourage the children to sound out the initial blend and word ending before saying the word. More able children could write a list of the words that they are building as they play.

AGE RANGE 6–7

LEARNING OBJECTIVE
To change medial letter patterns in a word and read a range of familiar words.

CURRICULUM LINKS
NLS: Y2, T1, Word level 1.

Shoot!

What you need
Three small foam balls; a marker pen.

What to do
● Use the marker pen to write one of the patterns *ee*, *ea* and *oo* on each of the three foam balls. Write the following list of words in a column on the board:

fed	red	hot	lop	hop
pop	slop	stop	shot	swap

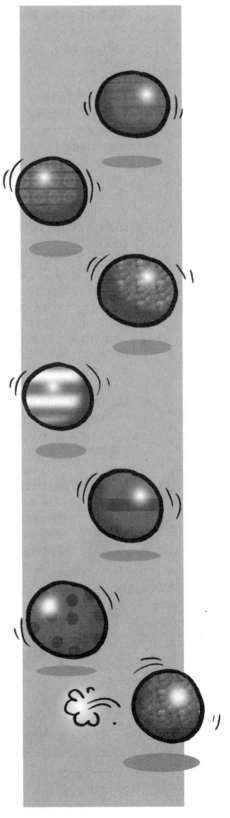

● Show the children the three balls, and tell them that they are going to play a game. Explain that first, you are going to make sure that they all know the sounds that these patterns make in words.
● Tell the children that you are going to throw a ball to one of them and they must give the sound for the pattern on that ball. Use all three balls in turn to give a number of children practice in reading the patterns. If a child gives the *oo* sound as in *book* for *oo*, explain that for this game you are focusing on the sound as in *moon*.
● Now explain that you are going to point to a word on the board and then throw a ball to someone. Say, *I want you to tell me what the word would be if we changed the vowel in the middle for the pattern on the ball.* Invite one or two children to try this, throwing the ball back to you as they give their answer.
● Now begin the game, making sure that you throw a ball with a pattern that will allow the child to build a real word from the word that you point to. Familiarise yourself with the following list of potential words to help the game go smoothly.

Fed: feed, food	swop: sweep, swoop
pop: peep, poop	hop: heap, hoop
slop: sleep, sloop	hot: heat, hoot
stop: steep, stoop	lop: leap, loop
shot: sheet, shoot	red: reed, read

● Use one ball to help the children create a number of new words, before changing to a ball with a different pattern. When the children are more confident, change the balls more frequently.

Differentiation
Rather than the original words, write a list of potential word pairs on the board for younger children. Point to the pair and throw the ball, asking the children to read the word that contains the pattern on the ball. Keep the pace of the game brisk for older children. Throw two balls with different patterns in succession to the same child, using the same cue word.

AGE RANGE 7–8

LEARNING OBJECTIVE
To practise making a choice between the *ee* and *ea* patterns in common words to spell the long *ee* phoneme.

CURRICULUM LINKS
NLS: to secure the spelling of each of the long vowel phonY3, T3, Word level 1.

Neat feet

What you need
The 'Neat feet' photocopiable sheet on page 93 (enough for two children to share); thin card; two sets of shoe and feet counters (see photocopiable); two dice; paper; pencils.

What to do
● Copy the photocopiable sheet onto thin card to make a game board. Cut out the two pairs of shoe and feet counters and stick them onto different colour card. Laminate the counters or cover them with self-adhesive plastic to make them more sturdy.
● Divide the children into pairs and give each pair a set of counters and a copy of the photocopiable sheet.
● Show the children the *ee* and the *ea* patterns on the shoe and feet counters, and ask them to tell you the sound that these patterns make. Explain that we often have to make a choice between these two patterns when spelling a word that contains an *ee* sound.
● Tell them that they are going to play in pairs and that they are going to take turns to throw the two dice and move their four counters around the board. Point out that they can only place their counter on a square if it will make a correctly spelled word. Place one of each type of counter on the board to illustrate this, indicating both a correct (*feed*) and incorrect spelling (*fead*). Show the children that, in some instances, both patterns would make a correct spelling (*meat/meet*, for example).
● Invite the children to throw one of the dice to decide who should go first, then let this player throw both dice. Explain that the two scores can be added together to move one counter only, or used separately to move two counters.
● As the game progresses it may be necessary to help the children try out the best way to use the scores. Encourage them to consider how far their counters can travel with the scores and whether they can make a correctly spelled word.
●The first player to complete the track with all four of their counters is the winner.

Differentiation
Provide a checklist of spellings that it is possible to make in the game, so that younger children can check whether they have placed a counter correctly to spell a word. As more able children play, encourage them to write down the words that they have made in two columns, under the headings *ee* and *ea*. In this version, there may be two winners – the player who completes the track first or the player who has made the greatest number of words.

Phonic Fun! **BRIGHT IDEAS**

AGE RANGE 7–8

LEARNING OBJECTIVE
To be able to use the correct sound of two alternatives for the same pattern when reading a range of words.

CURRICULUM LINKS
NLS: Y2, T3, Word level 6.

Sound snap

What you need
40 pieces of thin card measuring 5cm by 7cm; pen.

What to do
● On each piece of card write one of the following words:

snow	arrow	mower	own
glow	below	bowler	grown
blow	follow	snowing	thrown
flow	narrow	owner	shown
slow	tomorrow	towing	bowl
how	tower	brown	owl
now	power	drown	howl
cow	towel	clown	fowl
row	rowdy	gown	prowl
bow	drowsy	town	growl

● Invite four children to play the game. Show them the 'cow' card and the 'snow' card, asking them to read the two words. Ask them whether the *ow* pattern makes the same sound in both words.

● Explain that each of the cards in the pack has a word with an *ow* pattern written on it. Remind the children that this pattern can make two sounds. Alert them to the fact that there are two cards in the pack which can be read with either of the two sounds (*row* and *bow*).
● Check that all the children understand the rules of Snap. Explain that in this version of the game, they must decide whether the *ow* pattern makes the same sound in two words in a row. If it does, they should shout out *Snap!*
● Deal out the cards, and ask each child to put their pile of cards face down in front of them. In turn, invite each child to take the card from the top of their pile, turn it over and read the word out, before putting it face up in a pile in the middle of the table. Explain that no-one must call *Snap!* until the word has been read. Start the game, reminding the children that the winner is the player who has won the greatest number of cards at the end of the game.

Differentiation
Read through all of the cards with younger children before beginning the game, and make it clear which two cards can be read with either sound. After the game, encourage older children to group the cards according to the sound made by the *ow* pattern. Encourage them to sort the cards into smaller groups, based on where that sound comes in the word, or the letter following that sound. Urge them to try to notice common features.

AGE RANGE 7–9

LEARNING OBJECTIVE
To recognise a variety of patterns used to write the long vowel phonemes.

CURRICULUM LINKS
NLS: Y3, T3, Word level 2.

Vowel teams

What you need
Thin card (A4 size); pen; 30 pieces of card measuring 5cm by 7cm.

What to do
● On the A4 card, draw a game board using the illustration below as a guide. Make one photocopy of the game board for each child.
● Write one of the following words on each piece of card:

(set 1)	(set 2)	(set 3)	(set 4)	(set 5)
flake	please	slice	strode	flute
plain	greet	flight	groan	juice
stray	piece	spy	grown	threw
eight	receive	height	toe	through
grey	these	tie	though	spoon
break	stream	eye	stow	cute

● Invite three children to play the game. Show the children one card from each set of words, asking them to read the five words and to tell you the vowel sound that they can hear in each word. Explain that these long vowel sounds are all spelled in a number of different ways in English, and that in this game they will need to recognise a number of different spellings for each vowel sound.
● Shuffle all the cards well and place them face down on the table. In turn, invite each child to pick up a card and read the word out to the group. Explain that when they have read the word, they must tell everyone the vowel sound that they heard, and then place the card on the correct rectangle on their game board. Show them that there is a place on the board for each of the vowel sounds.
● Tell the children that the aim of the game is to collect a full set of vowel sounds – a vowel 'team' – but that they can put more than one card on each rectangle.
● Suggest that if the children have more than one card with a given vowel sound, and someone else has a card that they need to make a set, then they could swap. But if they exchange cards in this way, they must miss their turn at picking up a card.
● Ask the children to place full vowel teams at the side of their board as they complete them, explaining that the player with the most teams wins the game.

Differentiation
For younger children, restrict the spelling patterns used on the cards and make more cards with words using the more common patterns, or use CVC words and encourage discrimination of the short vowel sounds. (You could use the words listed in the 'Families' activity on page 73 for this.) For older children, make a playing board with spaces for short vowel sounds as well, and provide a mix of words in the pack, asking the children to collect short and long vowel 'families'.

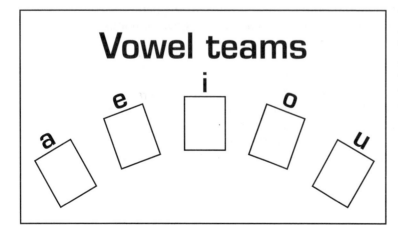

Phonic Fun! **BRIGHT IDEAS**

AGE RANGE 8–9

LEARNING OBJECTIVE
To recognise that pairs of words that sound the same may be written with different patterns and to correctly identify the meanings of each word in pairs of homophones.

CURRICULUM LINKS
NLS: Y4, T1, Word level 6.

Sound isn't everything

What you need
The 'Sound isn't everything: Judge's checklist' photocopiable sheet on page 94; 30 pieces of card measuring 5cm by 7cm; a pen.

What to do
● Write one homophone from the following list on each piece of card:

pane / pain	read / reed	ate / eight
main / mane	pale / pail	steal / steel
tale / tail	meet / meat	sale / sail
real / reel	heel / heal	toe / tow
write / right	vain / vane	peace / piece

● Invite three children to play the game. Show them one pair of homophone cards, asking them to read the words. Ask them whether the two words sound the same, and then whether they look the same. Invite them to tell you the meaning of each word. Remind them that pairs of words which sound the same but are spelled differently and have different meanings are called *homophones*. Explain that this word means *same sound*.

● Begin to lay out the pack of cards face down on the table in rows, telling the children that there are a number of pairs of homophones written on the back of the cards. Explain that two of the children are going to play against one another to see who can find the most homophones, and the third will act as a judge. Invite the children to decide who will be the judge, then hand the judge the checklist of meanings.

● Invite one of the players to turn over two cards and read the words. If the words do not sound the same, the player must turn them back over and let the next player have a turn. Encourage both players to try to remember the words that they read and where the cards were in the rows.

● If a player turns over a pair of homophones, then they should give the meaning of both words after reading them. The judge should then check whether the meanings that the player gave are correct. If they are, the player keeps the pair of cards and can turn over a second pair of cards. The winner is the player with the greatest number of homophone pairs when all of the cards have been picked up.

Differentiation
Limit the number of pairs used in the game at any one time for younger children. Read through all of the words first and also the relevant sentences from the checklist, pointing at the appropriate homophone in each sentence. Challenge older and more able children to create other homophone pairs cards to use in the game.

AGE RANGE 7–9

LEARNING OBJECTIVE
To remove the initial pattern from a given word and choose between a range of other initial patterns to construct new words.

CURRICULUM LINKS
NLS: Y4, T2, Word level 3.

Grab a Crab

What you need
The 'Grab a crab' photocopiable sheet on page 95; thin card; the 'Grab a crab playing cards' photocopiable sheet on page 96; red and black pens; paper; pencils.

What to do
● Copy the 'Grab a crab' photocopiable sheet onto card to make a game board. Make three copies of the 'Grab a crab playing cards' photocopiable onto thin card. Cut out the 27 crab cards, number them from 1 to 27, and write one of the following words on the back of each, using red pen for the initial letter or consonant cluster and black for the remainder of the word:

slap	swill	bring	blame	bright	stutter
trap	clump	cry	stay	round	crumble
brag	plank	happy	stain	clown	
crop	grand	freed	share	throw	
whip	think	flame	chair	mind	

● Invite three children to play the game. Give each child a piece of paper and a pencil. Place the playing cards face down on the table and ensure that the children have a good view of the game board.
● Explain that the children are going to take turns to pick up a card. They must look at the word on the card and then at each of the crabs on the board in turn. If they can use both of the initial patterns on a crab to replace the beginning of the word on their card to make two new real words, then they can 'grab that crab'.
● On their piece of paper, they should write down the number of the crab and the two new words that they have made. Explain that they are allowed to grab more than one crab on any one turn, but they must be able to use both initial patterns on a crab.
● The winner is the player who has built the most new words.

Differentiation
Let younger children work in pairs. Read the initial word to them and help them to delete the initial pattern and blend the ending with the new patterns. Use only a few cards, making the goal to discover which crab can be swapped to make the most words. At the end of the game, challenge older children to try to build rhyming strings starting with the words that they have made.

Phonic Fun! **BRIGHT IDEAS**

AGE RANGE 7–9

LEARNING OBJECTIVE
To choose the correct spelling pattern for the phonemes *ar*, *or* and *er*, to build a range of words.

CURRICULUM LINKS
NLS: Y4, T1, Word level 3.

Lucky dip

What you need
Dice; small stickers to stick to the sides of the dice; 30 pieces of thin card measuring 5cm by 7cm; a bag.

What to do
● Write one of the patterns *or*, *ar*, *er*, *ir*, *ur* on a sticker and stick them onto the dice. Stick a blank sticker onto the sixth side, and draw an asterisk on it.
● On each of the pieces of card write a word frame from the list below:

d_t	g_m	h_d	f_st	th_n	s_t
d_n	h_m	c_l	f_t	st_m	t_t
ch_m	b_d	f_l	p_t	al_m	sh_t
h_t	c_d	b_st	t_n	l_d	ch_t
ch_n	t_m	g_l	w_n	y_d	th_d

● Place all of the cards in the bag and choose up to six children to play the game. Invite each child to select five cards at random and to lay these out in front of them on the table.
● Tell the children that they are going to take turns to roll the dice. When they have rolled the dice, they must check whether they can use the pattern they have thrown in the middle of one of their word frames to make a word. If they can make a word, they can turn the relevant card face down. Explain that if they roll the asterisk, they can use it for any pattern. The winner is the first player to turn over all of their cards.
● Let each player have a trial throw of the dice to check that they understand what they must do. Now explain that having built a word, a player may choose to miss a chance to turn over their own card in order to turn an opponent's card back over to delay them winning.

Differentiation
Let younger children choose just three cards. Help them to sound out the words, indicating if a particular pattern is not the correct choice for the *er* phoneme. Extend the game by asking older children to construct a list of as many words as they can using their five word frames and any of the '*r* pair' patterns. Point out that it may be possible to use several patterns with any one frame.

AGE RANGE 9–11

LEARNING OBJECTIVE
To be able to distinguish when to double a consonant before the –*le* ending.

CURRICULUM LINKS
NLS: Y5, T1, Word level 3; Y6, T1, Word level 3.

Double or quits

What you need
A copy of the word pairs list below; whiteboard; pen.

What to do
● Write the words *scrabble*, *pebble*, *scribble*, *hobble* and *bubble* on the board. Remind the children that there is a spelling rule for words which end in –*le*. Explain that only a short vowel has a double consonant between itself and –*le*. Underline the double letters in the words as you say the vowel sounds.

● Use the word *ramble* to illustrate that no doubling is needed if there are already two consonants after the short vowel. Use *table*, *gargle* and *poodle* to demonstrate that other vowel sounds do not need a double consonant either.

● Now divide the children into two teams. Explain that you are going to go around the group, giving two words to one person at a time in each team (use *stable* and *babble* as an example). That person must say which of these words would have a double consonant to score a team point. Tell the children that if they are correct, you will invite the next person in their team to have a go. Each person can decide whether to try to answer or 'quit'. If someone quits, the pair of words passes to the other team. The winning team is the one with the most correct answers. Toss a coin to decide on the team that starts the game.

● Just before you begin, tell the children that there are two words in the game which break the rule. They are *triple* and *treble*. Write them on the board and repeat the words, explaining that they should have a double consonant. Erase them and begin the game.

● Use the following word pairs:

staple / grapple	dabble / cable	angle / straggle
toggle / ogle	noble / bobble	ripple / simple
bubble / bugle	idle / riddle	handle / rattle
stifle / sniffle	able / dabble	gaggle / gargle
needle / meddle	ruffle / rifle	hurdle / huddle
saddle / ladle	fable / rattle	triple / stipple
kettle / eagle	middle / noodle	bramble / rabble
steeple / topple	stable / bubble	bangle / battle
people / supple	cradle / fiddle	gurgle / giggle
title / brittle	ripple / simple	pebble / treble

Differentiation
With younger and less able children, focus only on the pairs which require the children to distinguish between a long and a short vowel sound at first, adding the other pairs later. Ask older and more able children to write down the word with the double letter on the whiteboard before the player gives an answer.

AGE RANGE 9–11

LEARNING OBJECTIVE
To practise a selection of rules for adding suffixes to common words.

CURRICULUM LINKS
NLS: Y5, T1, Word level 3; Y6, T1, Word level 3.

Drop it

What you need
16 pieces of pieces of thin card measuring 5cm by 7cm in one colour; 24 pieces of card in another colour; pen.

What to do
● Prepare the 16 instruction cards by writing one of the rules below on each card. Repeat each rule four times.
1) Just add
2) Replace the silent *e*
3) Change *y* to *i* and add
4) Double the final consonant and add
● On each of the playing cards write one of the following words:

have + ing	fly + ing	stop + ing
hate + ful	dry + er	land + ing
rose + y	cry + es	fit + ness
race + er	spy + ed	slip + y
late + ly	happy + ness	fat + er
safe + ty	marry + age	soak + ing
dine + ed	hurry + ing	trust + ful
care + less	merry +ment	jot + er

● Shuffle both sets of cards well, and invite four children to play the game.
● Place the set of rule cards face down on the table in a pile, then deal three of the word cards to each of the players. Suggest that the children lay out the cards in front of them on the table.
● Explain that the children are each going to pick up one of the rule cards in turn. If they have a word card for which the rule is appropriate, they can 'drop' that card and pick up another. Turn over the top rule card and use it as an example with one of the children's cards. Place it back on the bottom of pile, then invite the children to start playing.
● Explain that when all of the question cards have been used, the winner is the player who has 'dropped' the most cards.

Differentiation
With younger and less able children, recap on the rules for suffixing before beginning the game and let the children play in pairs, making joint decisions. For more able children, make extra sets of question cards to give practice of suffixing rules with a wider range of words.

AGE RANGE 9–11

LEARNING OBJECTIVE
To build common words in a given category from syllables.

CURRICULUM LINKS
NLS: Y5, T3, Word level 3; Y6, T1, Word level 3.

Syllable scramble

What you need
Pieces of card measuring 5cm square; blue, red and black pens; six envelopes.

What to do
● Write one of the following headings on each of the six envelopes:

1) Creatures: two syllables
2) Creatures: three syllables
3) Countries: two syllables
4) Countries: three syllables
5) Fruit and vegetables: two syllables
6) Fruit and vegetables: three syllables

● Now make up some sets of syllable cards. Write the initial syllable in blue pen, the second syllable in red pen and third syllables, where applicable, in black pen.
● Trim the card so that syllables will fit together without spaces to form words.

Creatures			Countries			Fruit and vegetables		
zeb	ger		Eng	and		ap	bage	
ti	key		Nor	ia		car	ry	
liz	affe		Holl	key		or	ple	
mon	ra		Tur	land		cab	rot	
gir	ard		Russ	way		cher	ange	
oc	e	ope	Ger	em	land	pot	i	choke
el	o	zee	Por	al	y	tom	at	ine
kan	tel	phant	Lux	ad	y	on	ti	o
chim	to	dile	lt	tu	bourg	cu	ger	to
croc	gar	pus	Switz	man	a	ar	cum	on
an	pan	oo	Can	er	gal	tan	a	ber

● Place each set in the relevant envelope.
● Choose one set of cards and lay them out on the table in the arrangement above.
● Invite two or three children to sort out the syllables into words. Explain that all of the words will be names of creatures, for example, and point out that the colour-coding will help them to build the syllables in the correct order.
● Work through each set of cards in the same way.

Differentiation
For younger and less able children, use the two-syllable words only and provide a checklist of correct words. Do not specify the category of words for older and more able children. Simply spread the syllables on the table without ordering them at all. Challenge the children to work out the significance of the different colours.

Round and Round the Garden

Five in a Hive

Finish

Start

Phonic Fun!   BRIGHT IDEAS

Round and Round the Garden

Five in a Hive

Line up

wool	stool	door	soot	food	spoon	poor
took	book	hoof	loop	wooden	cook	fool
hood	root	proof	nook	groom	gloom	stood
looked	rook	room	brook	good	goose	floor
noodle	hoop	shook	book	pool	bloom	wool
too	troop	foot	moon	look	noon	stoop
took	soon	soot	loop	loot	fool	snooze
roost	spoon	hoof	wood	boom	cook	crook
roof	moo	stool	poodle	poor	choose	troop
door	room	loose	brook	pool	wool	hood

Blend it

→ sl ____	tr ____	sn ____	br ____	bl ____	FINISH spr____
pr ____	pl ____	gr ____	sw ____	scr ____	← gl ____
→ dr ____	fl ____	thr ____		ch ____	fr ____
sh ____	sp ____	str ____	cl ____	cr ____	← th ____
→ sl ____	tr ____		br ____	bl ____	spr ____
pr ____	pl ____	gr ____	sn ____	sw ____	← scr ____
→ fl ____	thr ____	st ____	ch ____	fr ____	gl ____
dr ____	sh ____	sp ____	str ____	cl ____	← cr ____
START →	br ____	bl ____	spr ____	sn ____	th ____

Phonic Fun! BRIGHT IDEAS

Neat feet

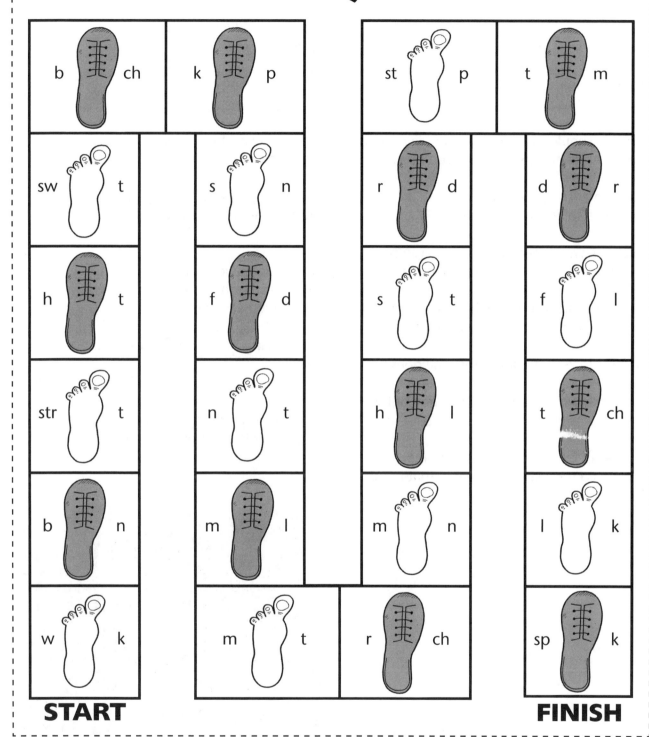

START

FINISH

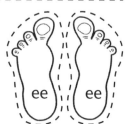

Sound isn't everything

Judge's checklist

The greedy boy ate too many sweets.
Two times four makes eight.

I have a blister on my heel.
The blister has begun to heal.

Children should not ride bikes on main roads.
She gave the horse's mane a good brush.

Meet me at the park tonight.
I eat vegetables but not meat.

I knew he was ill because he looked so pale.
She couldn't carry the heavy pail of water.

I broke a window pane with my football.
The boy had a terrible pain in his tummy.

She likes to read a book before she goes to
  sleep.
The frog hid in the reeds at the edge of the
  pond.

He doesn't believe that ghosts are real.
You should have seen him reel in that huge
  fish.

The boat had a blue sail.
I bought my new coat in the sale.

It is very wrong to steal.
The bridge was made of steel.

The dog wags his tail when he sees me.
My friend told me a very strange tale.

That man just stood on my toe.
We are waiting for a truck to tow our car
  home.

I must write a letter to my friend this evening.
Please turn right at the next corner.
His answer was right.

He's looking in the mirror again because he's
  so vain.
The weather vane turned round in the wind.

I can't get any peace in here.
Can I have the last piece of pie?

Grab a crab

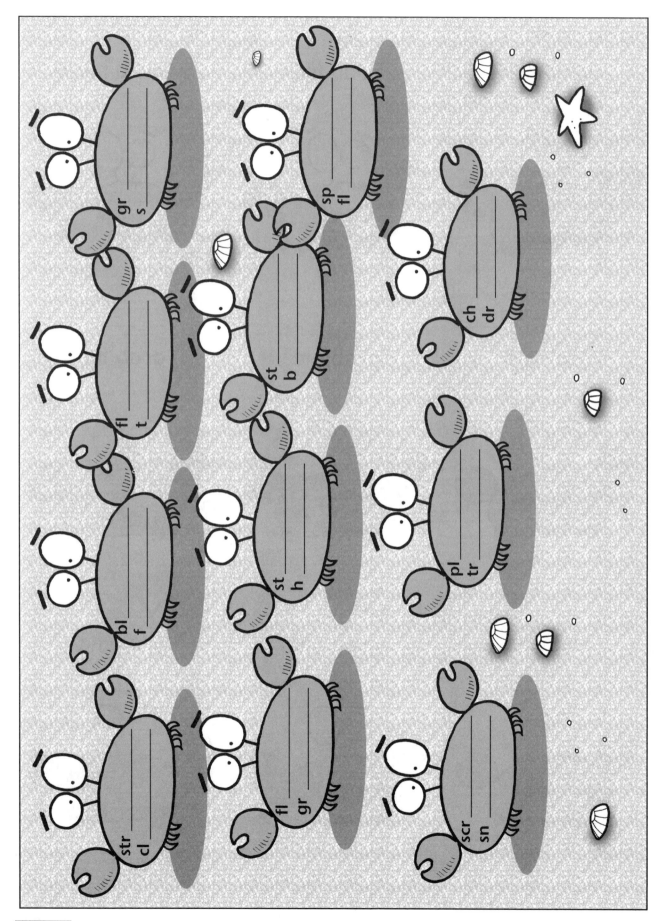

Grab a crab playing cards

grab me

grab me

grab me

grab me

grab me

grab me

grab me

grab me

grab me